Go and Be Reconciled
What Does This Mean?

A Bible Study on Reconciliation
Reviewing *Luther's Small Catechism*

Produced by

Ambassadors
of
Reconciliation™

P.O. Box 81662
Billings, MT 59108-1662 USA
www.HisAoR.org

Lifestyles of Reconciliation is a Bible study series designed to help God's people appreciate the gift of reconciliation that is theirs in Jesus Christ and to improve their service as Christ's ambassadors in everyday life (2 Corinthians 5:16-21). The ministry of reconciliation is given to the local church and every believer. Each of the studies in this series focuses on a different aspect of the believer's life. With the leader's notes included in every guide, these Bible studies may be used by individuals, small groups, retreats, or Sunday morning Bible classes. Visit our website for information on other studies – www.HisAoR.org.

Ambassadors of Reconciliation is a non-profit, international ministry founded to equip Lutherans and their churches for living, proclaiming, and cultivating lifestyles of reconciliation. We are a Recognized Service Organization of the Lutheran Church – Missouri Synod. Our approach is based upon the Holy Scriptures and the Lutheran Confessions. Learn more about us at www.HisAoR.org.

ISBN 978-0-9767874-9-5

Go and Be Reconciled:
What Does This Mean?

Contents

Note to Users of This Study

Go and Be Reconciled: What Does This Mean? is divided into six lessons, one lesson for each of the six chief parts of Christian doctrine as described in *Luther's Small Catechism.* It is not intended to replace confirmation courses. This study provides opportunity to review the fundamentals of the Christian faith while learning how these truths provide direction for daily life, especially in reconciliation.

This study has been developed for three different applications:
- As a Bible study for small and large groups
- As an independent study for individuals
- As an aid for coaching people struggling with specific conflicts, preparing them for reconciling with others on their own or through mediation

Note that each lesson likely will take 1.5 to 4 hours to complete in a Bible class format, depending on the amount of discussion utilized by participants. Because Bible study formats vary (from 45 minutes to 2+ hours per session), the number of sessions per lesson will vary.

As Bible study groups and leaders, take whatever time you desire. Allow for discussion time since much learning takes place while people are sharing their thoughts on particular topics.

The study is designed in a catechism format: Questions are presented for discussion, with multiple Bible passages providing insights from God's Word. The Leader's Notes in the back of this book are an integral part of the study, providing thoughts on how particular passages apply to each question.

Consider the following suggestions when planning your study.

Allow more than one session per lesson

- Expect that each lesson may require multiple sessions. Your group may take two or more sessions to cover each lesson.

Reduce amount of time spent on elements of each lesson

- The leader may assign different people to look up particular passages, saving time from having all participants look up every passage.
- The Bible study leader may limit the number of passages to look up during class, encouraging participants to look up the remainder on their own.
- The leader may assign some sections of each lesson as homework between group sessions.

Plan flexible use of case studies

Each lesson ends with an optional case study followed by application questions. Groups may decide not to utilize class time to discuss these cases. On the other hand, the case studies provide great opportunity to help participants apply the concepts to real life examples.

- As your group nears the end of the content sections, the leader may assign the reading of the case study for the next class. Ask participants to prepare for the next class by working through application questions for the case study.
- Use a half or full session to discuss the case thoroughly.
- Divide larger groups into small discussion groups to discuss the case study. Then ask a representative from each group to summarize key insights learned.
- Choose a few of the case studies to discuss more thoroughly rather than review all of them.

Go and Be Reconciled: What Does This Mean? can be used in multiple ways. Utilize this study in the way that best fits your needs and opportunities.

"Now may the God of peace who brought again from the dead our Lord Jesus, the great shepherd of the sheep, by the blood of the eternal covenant, equip you with everything good that you may do his will, working in us that which is pleasing in his sight, through Jesus Christ, to whom be glory forever and ever. Amen." (Hebrews 13:20-21)

Introduction: Go and Be Reconciled – *What Does This Mean?*

From the time that Adam and Eve first fell into sin, God's people have been in conflict – with Him and with one another. Throughout the Bible, God tells us how He reconciled us to Himself through the atoning work of Jesus Christ, His only Son. He further instructs us how to respond to our conflicts with others.

This study looks at two key components of reconciliation: reconciliation to God and reconciliation with others. In Scripture, God calls us to be reconciled:

> "We implore you on behalf of Christ, be reconciled to God" (2 Corinthians 5:20b).

> "[Jesus said,] 'First be reconciled to your brother, and then come and offer your gift'" (Matthew 5:24b).

Basic teachings from *Luther's Small Catechism* reflect God's ministry of reconciliation and how we ought to relate to God and to one another. Each lesson begins with a review of a chief part of Christian doctrine from *Luther's Small Catechism*. Not only will this serve as a refresher for many, but it also will serve to demonstrate how reconciliation is meant to be a way of life for the child of God.

Following the catechism review, a number of questions are posed to guide the Bible student in reflection on reconciliation. This study is divided into six lessons: Three each for "Be Reconciled to God" and "Be Reconciled to Others."

At the end of each lesson is a short case study with application questions. The case study can be used for class (or small group) discussions led by the application questions.

In addition, the application questions can be useful in guiding you to address a specific conflict. Consider an actual conflict from your life. Answer the application questions, applying them to your specific situation. Write down your answers to the questions:

- Writing your answers helps you think more specifically and practically.
- Written answers are easier to review later on, whether on your own or with someone who may be coaching you.
- Written answers prepare you when going to be reconciled, planning specific words you can say to the person with whom you are in conflict.

This study is divided into two main parts: "Be Reconciled to God" and "Be Reconciled to Others." Each part has three lessons as outlined below.

Be Reconciled to God
2 Cor. 5:18-20

Remember Whose You Are
How does my identity affect reconciliation?

Repent Before God
How do my conflicts with others affect my relationship with God?

Receive God's Forgiveness
How am I reconciled to God?

Be Reconciled to Others
Matt. 5:23-24

Confess to the Other Person
How does my confession lead to reconciliation?

Forgive as God Forgave You
How does forgiving and resolving lead to reconciliation?

Restore with Gentleness
How does restoring others lead to reconciliation?

The cross can remind us how we are reconciled. In our vertical relationship, God reconciled us to Himself through Christ. We remember that we are His children, called to a lifestyle of repentance, receiving His forgiveness. In our horizontal relationship, we are called to be reconciled with other people for whom Christ has died. We confess our sins to the other person, forgive as God forgave us through Christ, and restore others with gentleness.

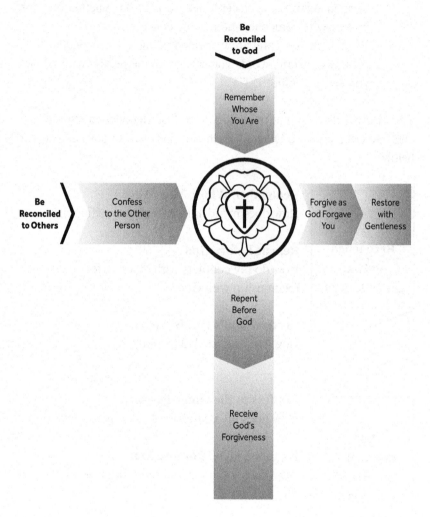

Prayer: Heavenly Father, You reconciled me to You through Your only Son while I was still a sinner. In this study, guide me to be reconciled with others as You have reconciled me to You through Christ. Help me learn not just theory but how to apply Your Word in my relationships with others. Encourage me through the power of your forgiveness to do that which I could never do on my own – so that with the Apostle Paul, I can confess with confidence, "I can do all things through Christ who strengthens me." In Jesus' name, Amen.

Be Reconciled to God

1: Remember Whose You Are

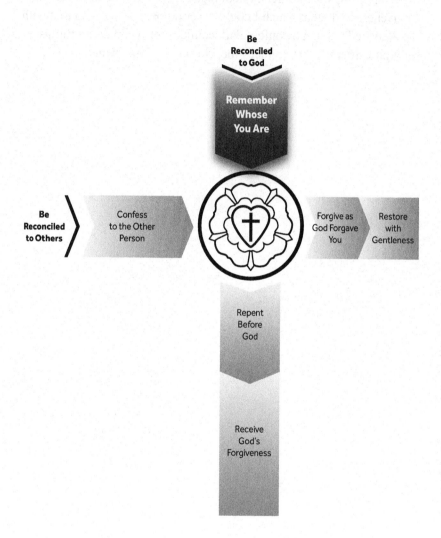

Be
Reconciled
to God

Remember
Whose
You Are

Be
Reconciled
to Others

Confess
to the Other
Person

Forgive as
God Forgave
You

Restore
with
Gentleness

Repent
Before
God

Receive
God's
Forgiveness

What does it mean to be reconciled to God?
2 Corinthians 5:18-20

1: Remember Whose You Are.

How does my identity affect reconciliation?

Luther's Small Catechism teaches that in our Baptism we were given a new identity. This identity affects how we view ourselves and others, including during our disagreements. Remembering our Baptism reminds us whose we are.

 Review from *Luther's Small Catechism*:
The Sacrament of Holy Baptism

As the head of the family should teach it in a simple way to his household

First

What is Baptism?

Baptism is not just plain water, but it is the water included in God's command and combined with God's word.

Which is that word of God?

Christ our Lord says in the last chapter of Matthew: "Therefore go and make disciples of all nations, baptizing them in the name of the Father and of the Son and of the Holy Spirit." (Matthew 28:19)

Second

What benefits does Baptism give?

It works forgiveness of sins, rescues from death and the devil, and gives eternal salvation to all who believe this, as the words and promises of God declare.

Which are these words and promises of God?

Christ our Lord says in the last chapter of Mark: "Whoever believes and is baptized will be saved, but whoever does not believe will be condemned." (Mark 16:16)

Third

How can water do such great things?

Certainly not just water, but the word of God in and with the water does these things, along with the faith which trusts this word of God in the water. For without God's word the water is plain water and no Baptism. But with the word of God it is a Baptism, that is, a life-giving water, rich in grace, and a washing of the new birth in the Holy Spirit, as St. Paul says in Titus, chapter three:

> "He saved us through the washing of rebirth and renewal by the Holy Spirit, whom He poured out on us generously through Jesus Christ our Savior, so that, having been justified by His grace, we might become heirs having the hope of eternal life. This is a trustworthy saying." (Titus 3:5-8)

Fourth

What does such baptizing with water indicate?

It indicates that the Old Adam in us should by daily contrition and repentance be drowned and die with all sins and evil desires, and that a new man should daily emerge and arise to live before God in righteousness and purity forever.

Where is this written?

St. Paul writes in Romans chapter six: "We were therefore buried with Him through baptism into death in order that, just as Christ was raised from the dead through the glory of the Father, we too may live a new life." (Romans 6:4)

Who Am I by nature?

Watch a young child to see what happens when she doesn't get what she wants. What are some things she might do in response to not getting her way?

Where does she learn to handle things this way?

1. The Bible teaches who we are by nature. Discuss how the following Scripture passages describe our old identity and the consequences of this nature.

By nature, I am:

- A sinful creature.
  - Psalm 51:5
  - Romans 3:10-12; 23
  - James 2:10

- An enemy of God.
  - Isaiah 59:2
  - Romans 5:10

- One who daily struggles with my sinful nature.
  - Job 14:4; 15:14
  - Romans 7:14-25
  - Galatians 5:17

- Unclean and worthless, a beggar who has nothing to offer God.
  - Isaiah 64:6
  - Romans 3:12
  - 1 Timothy 6:7

- Condemned to be separated from God eternally.
  - Romans 6:23a

Who Am I in Christ?

When his teenage daughters began going out on their own, their father said to them as they were going out the door, "Remember who you are." What do you think he was telling them?

2. In spite of our sinful nature, we have been given a new nature as children of God. What are the benefits of this new nature, based on the passages that follow?

In Christ, I am:

- A new creature through Him.
  - Isaiah 53:5-6
  - John 3:16
  - 2 Corinthians 5:16-21

- In Baptism changed from an enemy to an heir.
  - Romans 6:2-5
  - Galatians 3:26-4:7
  - Titus 3:5-7

- A beloved child of God, precious in His eyes.
  - Isaiah 43:4
  - John 1:12-13
  - 1 John 3:1

- Cleansed and ransomed by the precious blood of Christ.
  - 1 John 1:7
  - 1 Peter 1:18-19

- No longer separated from God. I have been brought near by His blood.
  - Ephesians 2:12-13
  - Romans 8:35-39

3. Reflecting on these verses, how can I understand my worth as an individual?

4. What difference does that make when we suffer from the effects of a serious conflict?
   - Joshua 1:5
   - Colossians 3:12-17

What does my Baptism have to do with conflict?

Conflict often catches us by surprise, leading us to react immediately without thinking. As Christians, we should anticipate conflict because we live in a world tainted by sin, and people are sinful by nature. Knowing what God has done for us through Christ, the Bible teaches us to respond to conflict in ways that are dramatically different from our sinful nature.

Consider how reflecting on one's Baptism through the following verses might affect the way you respond to conflict:

5. My Baptism comforts me through the _____

    of _____ and the gift of the Holy Spirit. My

    _____ have been washed away.
    • Acts 2:38; 22:16

6. Baptism gives me my identity as a new _____

    and a _____ of _____.
    • 2 Corinthians 5:17
    • 1 John 3:1

7. Baptism reminds me that I am called to live not for

    _____ but rather for _____.
    • 2 Corinthians 5:14-15

8. Having been baptized into Christ, I can walk in the

    _____ of life.
    • Romans 6:3-4

9. Baptism teaches me to put off the _____ _____

    and put on a _____ _____.
    • Ephesians 4:22-24
    • Review "*What does such baptizing with water indicate?*"
      from the catechism section at the beginning of this lesson.

Luther instructs that before our prayers in the morning and when we
go to bed, we should "Make the sign of the holy cross and say: In the
name of the Father and of the ✠ Son and of the Holy Spirit. Amen."

10. How does this remind me of my Baptism?

11. How might making the sign of the cross affect my attitude if I
    did this before responding to a conflict?

Who needs to be reconciled?

Identify the parties to be reconciled and how we should view them.

12. First, I need to be reconciled to _____.
    - Psalm 51:3-5
    - 1 John 1:8-9

13. Next, I need to be reconciled to others:

    Someone who has something against _____.
    - Matthew 5:23-24

    Someone who has sinned against _____.
    - Matthew 18:15

14. Whether or not I need to be reconciled to someone else,

    I may need to help a brother or sister in Christ who is

    _____ in sin. However, I must use care to

    restore in a spirit of gentleness so that I also may not be

    _____ to sin.
    - Galatians 6:1-2

15. I should view others in conflict as people for whom

    _____ _____ _____.
    - John 3:16
    This includes:
    - A brother or sister in Christ (a fellow child of God).
      - 1 John 3:1, 23
    - Someone who does not yet know Christ.
      - 1 Peter 2:12
      - 1 Peter 3:14-17

What is the difference between *conflict resolution* and *reconciliation*?

In *conflict resolution*, we address the *material* or *substantive* issues of the conflict. Examples include issues involving money, property, roles, structure, etc. We identify the problems to be solved and negotiate with the other person to resolve them.

In *reconciliation*, we seek to restore the relationship by addressing the *relational* or *personal* issues of the conflict. Examples include such things as hurtful words and actions, gossip, avoidance, denial, etc. Relational issues are reconciled through confession and forgiveness.

16. My most serious conflict in all of life is with _____.
    • Isaiah 59:2
    • Romans 3:10-12

17. The consequence of being in conflict with God is

    _____.
    • Romans 6:23a

18. In addressing my conflict with Him, God chose

    _____ (*conflict resolution* or *reconciliation*).
    • 2 Corinthians 5:18-19

19. Which is more difficult – *conflict resolution* or *reconciliation*? Why?

 Case Study

Robert and Emily, adult siblings, disagree on how to provide care for their elderly mother, Esther. Esther has been living alone in her home, but her health has been declining over the last few years. Five weeks ago she fell and broke her hip. After a week in the hospital, she has been in a recovery center receiving care and therapy. Esther is ready to be released but cannot stay in her home alone anymore.

Years before (while Dad was living), Robert promised both his parents that he would never put them into a nursing home. Robert wants Mom to live with her children trading every other month – one month with Robert and his wife, and the next month with Emily and her husband. Emily believes that Mom should be moved into a permanent nursing facility where she can receive 24-hour care. Emily is worried that neither of them can provide the kind of care their mother needs. Esther wants to move back into her home. She knows that is not possible now, but she hopes that soon she can return home.

Emily and Robert have had a number of disagreements over the care of their mother, but on the day before Esther was to be released, they both lost their tempers in front of the social worker. Emily called her brother stupid and unrealistic. Robert accused his sister of being non-caring and unwilling to sacrifice for their mother. No decision was reached, and they left the social worker's office still bickering.

Esther, Robert and his wife, and Emily and her husband are all Christians, but Emily's family attends a different church.

 Application

These questions can apply to the above case study or to a current conflict from your personal life. For the case study, you can assume either Robert's or Emily's role. For a conflict from your life, apply these questions to yourself, writing out your answers.

1. How have you contributed to this conflict? Who has been affected by your sinful thoughts, words, or actions?

2. In spite of your sinful nature, how does your heavenly Father view:
    a. you?
    b. the person with whom you are in conflict?

3. In light of how your heavenly Father views you both:
   a. What is your worth to God?
   b. What is the other person's worth to God?

4. Review the catechism question, "What benefits does Baptism give?" on page 11. What comfort does your Baptism give you in the midst of this struggle?

5. In Christ, we are called as new creatures to put away our "old self" and put on our "new self" in Christ.
   a. How can you put away your old self in this conflict?
   b. How can you put on your new self in Christ?
   c. What would your contrition and repentance look like?

6. Describe what material or substantive issues need to be resolved in your conflict.

7. Identify what relational issues need to be reconciled in your conflict.

8. Write a prayer asking for God's help in resolving the material issues and reconciling with the other person.

Be Reconciled to God
2: Repent Before God

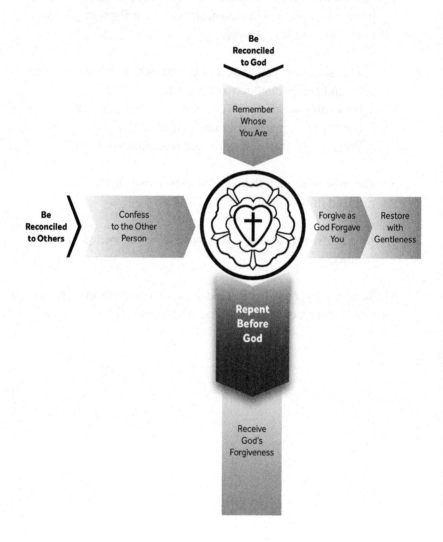

What does it mean to be reconciled to God?
2 Corinthians 5:18-20

2: Repent Before God

How do my conflicts with others affect my relationship with God?

Reconciliation continues as we examine ourselves according to the Ten Commandments.

 Review from *Luther's Small Catechism:*
The Ten Commandments

As the head of the family should teach it in a simple way to his household

The First Commandment
You shall have no other gods.
> *What does this mean?* We should fear, love, and trust in God above all things.

The Second Commandment
You shall not misuse the name of the Lord your God.
> *What does this mean?* We should fear and love God so that we do not curse, swear, use satanic arts, lie, or deceive by His name, but call upon it in every trouble, pray, praise, and give thanks.

The Third Commandment
Remember the Sabbath day by keeping it holy.
> *What does this mean?* We should fear and love God so that we do not despise preaching and His Word, but hold it sacred and gladly hear and learn it.

The Fourth Commandment
Honor your father and your mother.
> *What does this mean?* We should fear and love God so that we do not despise or anger our parents and other authorities, but honor them, serve and obey them, love and cherish them.

The Fifth Commandment
You shall not murder.
> *What does this mean?* We should fear and love God so that

we do not hurt or harm our neighbor in his body, but help and support him in every physical need.

The Sixth Commandment

You shall not commit adultery.

> *What does this mean?* We should fear and love God so that we lead a sexually pure and decent life in what we say and do, and husband and wife love and honor each other.

The Seventh Commandment

You shall not steal.

> *What does this mean?* We should fear and love God so that we do not take our neighbor's money or possessions, or get them in any dishonest way, but help him to improve and protect his possessions and income.

The Eighth Commandment

You shall not give false testimony against your neighbor.

> *What does this mean?* We should fear and love God so that we do not tell lies about our neighbor, betray him, slander him, or hurt his reputation, but defend him, speak well of him, and explain everything in the kindest way.

The Ninth Commandment

You shall not covet your neighbor's house.

> *What does this mean?* We should fear and love God so that we do not scheme to get our neighbor's inheritance or house, or get it in a way which only appears right, but help and be of service to him in keeping it.

The Tenth Commandment

You shall not covet your neighbor's wife, or his manservant or maidservant, his ox or donkey, or anything that belongs to your neighbor.

> *What does this mean?* We should fear and love God so that we do not entice or force away our neighbor's wife, workers, or animals, or turn them against him, but urge them to stay and do their duty.

The Close of the Commandments

What does God say about all these commandments? He says: "I, the LORD your God, am a jealous God, punishing the children for the sin of the fathers to the third and fourth generation of those who hate Me, but showing love to a thousand generations of those who love Me and keep My commandments." (Exodus 20:5-6)

What does this mean? God threatens to punish all who break these commandments. Therefore, we should fear His wrath and not do anything against them. But He promises grace and every blessing to all who keep these commandments. Therefore, we should also love and trust in Him and gladly do what He commands.

What is the underlying source of our conflicts?

Conflict may be caused by misunderstandings or differences in perspectives or goals. But the Bible teaches that our fights and quarrels are caused by a certain kind of desire. Read James 4:1-3.

1. Not all desires are sinful. What kind of desires is James describing? How do these desires relate to the temptation in Genesis 3:5?

2. What does this indicate to you about life's daily conflicts in which we find ourselves?

What does conflict reveal about my heart?

Our quarrels and fights reveal our hidden desires, which become evident when we act on those desires and sin against God or others. Rather than responding to disagreements as children of God, we may react from our sinful nature by attacking or fleeing. When we don't get what we want, we make our demands known and punish others. For example:

- A teenager who is told he can't go to a certain party yells at his parents, calls them "dictators," and runs to his room slamming his door (attacking with hurtful words and attitude, then fleeing – avoiding his parents and denying his sin).

- A worker's request to take time off is declined, and she takes 2 hours during work to send texts to co-workers complaining about her boss and calling her boss names (fleeing by not addressing her concerns directly with her boss, then attacking through sinful complaints to others).

- A husband curses at his wife and storms out the door without telling her where he is going because she spent money on new clothes without talking to him. He wanted to buy a new TV (initially attacking through angry words, then fleeing instead of reconciling through confession and forgiveness).

3. In the examples above, explain how they all sinned against the First Commandment. Which of the other commandments were broken by the teenager, the worker, and the husband? (Note the explanations to the Commandments.)

4. These examples demonstrate how people might sin when they don't get what they want. Each one struggled with the "desires that battle within." According to the following verses, where does sin originate?
   - Psalm 51:10
   - Jeremiah 17:9-10
   - Matthew 15:19

How does conflict in my heart relate to idolatry?

Luther explains the First Commandment: "We should fear, love, and trust in God above all things." Any time we fear, love, or trust someone or something else more than God, we sin against this First Commandment. We are guilty of a form of idolatry, putting someone or something above God.

In *Luther's Large Catechism*, he expands the explanation to this Commandment: "A god is that to which we look for all good and in which we find refuge in every time of need. To have a god is nothing else than to trust and believe him with our whole heart. As I have often said, the trust and faith of the heart alone make both God and an idol…. That to which your heart clings and entrusts itself is, I say, really your God."[1]

5. Based on the *Small Catechism* explanation to the First Commandment, what are three ways in which we can sin against the First Commandment? Is it sinful to fear, love, or trust someone or something other than God?

6. Why would such fears, cravings, or misplaced trusts be described as idols?

When we are willing to sin in order to get what we want, we are not fearing God most of all. We are not loving Him above everyone or everything else. We are not trusting that He will give us everything we need. We turn our desires into demands – demanding what we want from others and even from God. This puts us in conflict with anyone (including God!) whom we believe is putting up a roadblock to our desires. The result? Fights and quarrels (James 4:1-3). Our heart is determined to get what we want, when we want it, and the way in which we want it.

When an individual behaves sinfully against another person, especially one who is close to him/her, the underlying motivation to serve one's own desires is revealed. Instead of self-sacrifice, one sacrifices the desires or needs of others, including other family members. Rather than restraining sinful thoughts, words, and actions, a person by nature falls prey to temptation to do whatever is necessary to please oneself.

Sinful behaviors exhibited in conflict reveal our struggle to serve ourselves and the secret desires of our hearts. We want to be the god of our own heart's desires, and we expect others to give in to our demands. In other words, we are guilty of idolatry!

---

1 Luther's Large Catechism, First Part: The Ten Commandments in Theodore E. Tappert, ed., *The Book of Concord: The Confessions of the Evangelical Lutheran Church* (Philadelphia: Fortress Press, 1959), 365.

What are some of the idols of the heart?

Sin originates in the heart. Our heart's desires become idolatrous when we fear, love, or trust someone or something more than God. Consider some of the idols of our hearts that might be revealed in conflict.

Improper desires for physical pleasure

Desires for physical pleasure are not necessarily sinful. God created us to enjoy His creation with its many pleasures. However, our sinful nature can take our God-given desires to an extreme, leading us to sin against God and others in order to satisfy these desires. The Bible refers to them as "cravings" or "lusts of the flesh."

7. How do the following Scripture verses describe these cravings?
    • 1 John 2:15-17
    • Galatians 5:16-21
    • Ephesians 4:17-20

We make a desire sinful (craving or lust) when we demand what we want. We think or act as if we simply must have it. We may be struggling with such an idol when we say, "Look, all I want is...!"

8. Give some examples of improper desires for physical pleasure that lead to conflict in our relationships.

9. Besides the First Commandment, what other Commandments would be broken in your examples?

Pride and arrogance

Pride is one of the most basic idols that can drive a person to sin. Scripture warns against pride and arrogance.

10. What are the consequences of this idol?
    • Proverbs 8:13
    • Proverbs 16:18
    • Matthew 23:12

Pride is part of the process of making one's self a "god." The prideful person exhibits self-centered thinking that can be expressed by, "I want it done my way, in my time, when I want it!"

Self-proclaimed "gods" judge others who do not meet their demands. These judgments lead to condemning and punishing those who do not serve them.

11. What does James call those who judge others in James 4:11-12?

12. How does gossip reflect the idols of pride and arrogance? Which Commandment is broken in gossip?

13. How is gossip a sin against the First Commandment? Who is the false god?

Love of money or material possessions
This form of idolatry is common among people. It's so easy for our hearts to yearn for money or material possessions.

14. What are the dangers of this idol? Consider the following:
   • 1 Timothy 6:10
   • Hebrews 13:5

15. The Bible identifies these also as cravings or lusts. This particular idol commonly leads to conflict, especially in marriage and the workplace. Give some examples where love of money or material possessions can lead to conflict in our relationships.

Fear of man
A healthy attitude includes caring about what others think of us. Such an outlook is important in developing and maintaining relationships. But when we exhibit an excessive concern about what others think of us, this reveals another idol. Being overly anxious about what others think is called "fear of man." This idol can lead to a preoccupation with acceptance, approval, popularity, personal comparisons, self-image, or pleasing others.

16. How do the Scriptures contrast the fear of man with the fear of God?
    - Proverbs 29:25
    - Luke 12:4-7

This idol is revealed when we act out of fear or anxiety about what others think of us. We might do something that we know is not right just to gain others' approval. The attitudes of "I just want to be accepted by others!" or "I just like to please everyone!" lead us to do sinful things just so that we will be accepted or liked by people. Peer pressure is a form of fear of man.

17. Give some examples of fear of man that lead to conflict.

Good things that I want too much
Some of the most difficult idols to deal with are the good desires that we elevate into demands. We all want good things that are blessings from God. However, when we turn our desires for good things into demands, we cross the line. We sin in order to satisfy our wants for good things. Again, these are described in the Bible as cravings or lusts.

18. Considering the following passages, identify good desires that might become idolatrous. How would you recognize when those desires turn into idols?
    - Luke 12:22-31
    - James 4:1-3

This idol may be revealed by worry or demands for a certain outcome. We may justify it by saying, "Look, all I want is..." Instead of depending on God for all our needs, we force things to go our way.

19. Provide some examples of good things that we want so badly that create strife in our relationships.
20. Besides the First Commandment, what other Commandments would be broken in your examples?

How do idols develop?

Notice that an idol can begin with a godly fear, desire, or trust. But once we demand what we want, it begins to develop into a full-blown idol. We slide down a slippery slope, moving from desire to demand. When expectations are not met, our frustration increases and we judge those who will not give us what we want. If they continue to refuse us, we punish them.

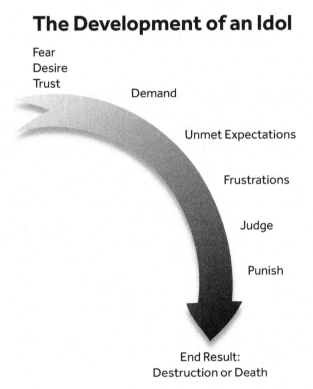

The Development of an Idol

Fear
Desire
Trust

Demand

Unmet Expectations

Frustrations

Judge

Punish

End Result:
Destruction or Death

21. What warning is found in Jonah 2:8?

22. What does God instruct in 1 John 5:21?

The devil promises good things (i.e., happiness, satisfaction, safety, success, fame, special knowledge, etc.) if we turn our devotion away from God and devote ourselves to the idols of our hearts. But this is a great deception!

If left unchecked, idolatry results in destruction or death of the idol and/or the person worshipping it. In other words, idolatry leads to death.

For example, consider the eventual results of a drug addict not giving up his cravings – loss of friends and family, loss of self-respect, loss of health . . . If he never gives up his craving for drugs, he will eventually lose his life. The use of the drug promised great feelings and freedom. In the end, however, it results in death.

Not everyone is a drug addict! But our own idols can lead to similar results.

What is sacrificed to the idols of our heart?

Those guilty of worshipping idols sacrifice to them. This is also true of idols of the heart. We sacrifice people or things to serve our own idols.

Consider a person whose idol was to get promoted at work. Janet believed that she deserved the promotion because of the number of years she worked for the company, and she wanted to earn more money. She had been overlooked for several promotions. When an opening for a higher position became available, Janet applied for it. But she learned that two co-workers also applied. Desperate to get the new position, she told some false rumors to the employer about the other two candidates, hoping that this would undermine their credibility and improve her odds for getting the job.

23. What did she sacrifice to achieve what she wanted?

The employer learned that the rumors were false. The woman not only failed to get the promotion, but she was terminated for her lack of integrity. Notice the progression of her idol:

The Development of an Idol *(Janet's Case)*

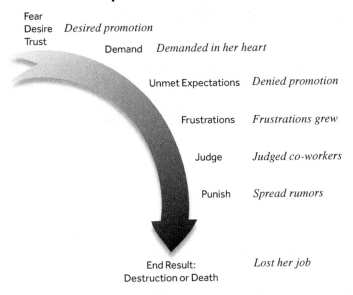

Fear
Desire   *Desired promotion*
Trust
              Demand   *Demanded in her heart*

              Unmet Expectations   *Denied promotion*

              Frustrations   *Frustrations grew*

              Judge   *Judged co-workers*

              Punish   *Spread rumors*

End Result: *Lost her job*
Destruction or Death

- Janet's original desire for a promotion was a good desire.
- However, her desire for a promotion turned into a demand – she just had to get this promotion.
- Her expectations were not met when she was not promoted earlier.
- Her frustrations grew each time she was not promoted, resulting in sinful anger.
- She judged her co-workers as threats to her opportunity to get this promotion.
- She punished her co-workers by spreading false rumors about them.

In the end, Janet's craving for a new job led her to sacrifice her own integrity, her witness to Christ, and her reputation. She not only failed to get the promotion, she lost her job. The development of her idol led to her own destruction.

24. Using the diagram "The Development of an Idol," describe how our own godly fears, desires, or trusts can develop into idols, leading us down the same path as Janet.

How can we flee from the idols of our hearts and turn towards God?

God calls us to repent of our sin, including the idols of our hearts. Through repentance, we exchange our worship of our false gods for the worship of the true God.

> 25. What does God require for sacrifice, according to Psalm 51:17?

The way to flee from our idols and turn towards God is this: Repent! Confess your sins to God and believe in His forgiveness for you!

> 26. How do the following passages provide comfort for your sins and hope for overcoming temptation?
> - Psalm 51:1-12
> - 1 John 1:9
> - 2 Corinthians 5:14-15
> - 1 Peter 2:24

 Case Study

Review the Case Study from Lesson 1 (page 17).

 Application

Put yourself into either Robert's or Emily's shoes. Use the questions below to understand his or her idols.

For personal application, consider a conflict where you may have felt one of the following: anger, bitterness, pride, fear, judgmental attitude, jealousy, or defensiveness. Reflect on the following questions to identify your underlying idols.

Consider the idols listed in this lesson. Ask yourself the following questions to identify the idols with which you were struggling:

1. Improper desires for physical pleasure
   a. What physical pleasure did you find yourself thinking about much of the time?
   b. When a certain desire or expectation was not met, did you feel frustration, resentment, bitterness, or anger?
   c. What was unsatisfying about the gifts God has given you?
   d. How did you get even with the other person when you did not get what you wanted from him/her?

2. Pride and arrogance
   a. How are your expectations of the other person magnifying your demands on him/her and your disappointment in his/her failure to meet your desires?
   b. How are you judging the other person when your desires are not met?
   c. How are you getting even with the other person when your desires are not met?
   d. How have you communicated to the other person what you feel he/she must do?
   e. How have you threatened the other person? ("Give me what I want or you will pay!")

3. Love of money or material possessions
   a. What preoccupies your thoughts? (What is the first thing on your mind in the morning and/or the last thing at night?)
   b. Fill in this blank: "If only I had _____, then I would be happy, fulfilled, and secure." What does this suggest to you about your trust in God for what you desire?
   c. When a certain desire or expectation is not met, do you feel frustration, resentment, bitterness, or anger?

4. Fear of man
   a. Whose approval do you want most of all?
   b. Whom are you seeking to please at almost any cost?
   c. What do you want to preserve or avoid about your reputation?
   d. In this situation, what or whom do you fear most?

5. Good things that I want too much
   a. What do you find yourself thinking about much of the time?
   b. What causes you the most worry? How has your anxiety replaced your trust in God?
   c. Fill in this blank: "If only _____, then I would be happy, fulfilled, and secure." What does this suggest to you about your trust in God for what you desire?
   d. When a certain desire or expectation is not met, do you feel frustration, resentment, bitterness, or anger?

6. What or whom have you sacrificed to get what you wanted?

7. If you do not repent of this pattern, what will be the destructive results?

8. What are some of the Commandments you have broken in this conflict? (Compare your thoughts, words, and actions to the explanations of the Ten Commandments.)

9. What hope is there for you? (See 1 John 1:9; Romans 5:8, 15:13; Ephesians 1:7.)

10. Write a prayer that reflects your confession and your thanks to God for His forgiveness. Include a petition for strength to overcome these temptations in the future.

Be Reconciled to God

3: Receive God's Forgiveness

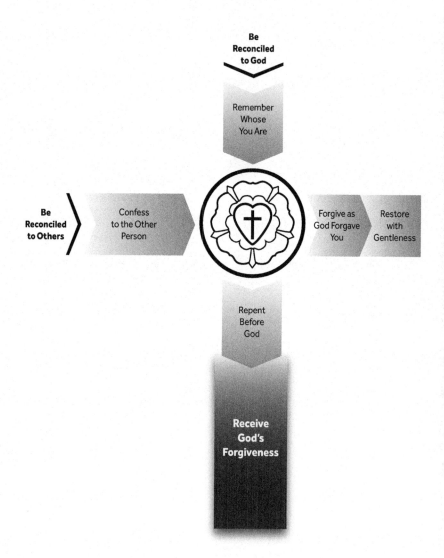

What does it mean to be reconciled to God?

2 Corinthians 5:18-20

3: Receive God's Forgiveness

How am I reconciled to God?

We consider reconciliation as we review confession and forgiveness.

 Review from *Luther's Small Catechism*:
Confession

As the head of the family should teach it in a simple way to his household

What is Confession?

Confession has two parts.

First, that we confess our sins, and
second, that we receive absolution, that is, forgiveness, from the pastor as from God Himself, not doubting, but firmly believing that by it our sins are forgiven before God in heaven.

What sins should we confess?

Before God we should plead guilty of all sins, even those we are not aware of, as we do in the Lord's Prayer; but before the pastor we should confess only those sins which we know and feel in our hearts.

Which are these?

Consider your place in life according to the Ten Commandments: Are you a father, mother, son, daughter, husband, wife, or worker? Have you been disobedient, unfaithful, or lazy? Have you been hot-tempered, rude, or quarrelsome? Have you hurt someone by your words or deeds? Have you stolen, been negligent, wasted anything, or done any harm?

[Luther provided a form for private confession as an example in the Small Catechism. For a contemporary form, refer to the pamphlet *Proclaiming God's Forgiveness* included in this study.]

What is the Office of the Keys?*

The Office of the Keys is that special authority which
Christ has given to His church on earth to forgive the sins
of repentant sinners, but to withhold forgiveness from the
unrepentant as long as they do not repent.

Where is this written?*

This is what St. John the Evangelist writes in chapter twenty:
The Lord Jesus breathed on His disciples and said, "Receive
the Holy Spirit. If you forgive anyone his sins, they are
forgiven; if you do not forgive them, they are not forgiven."
(John 20:22-23)

What do you believe according to these words?*

I believe that when the called ministers of Christ deal with
us by His divine command, in particular when they exclude
openly unrepentant sinners from the Christian congregation
and absolve those who repent of their sins and want to do
better, this is just as valid and certain, even in heaven, as if
Christ our dear Lord dealt with us Himself.

* This question may not have been composed by Luther himself but
reflects his teaching and was included in editions of the catechism
during his lifetime.

How does our idolatry lead us into more sin?

In Lesson 2, we reviewed the Ten Commandments and examined
how our sinful behaviors originate in the heart. The Bible teaches that
selfish desires lead to our fights and quarrels. We saw how idols begin
in the heart and lead us to slide down a slippery slope of sin.

One of the well known persons from the Old Testament is David,
the shepherd boy blessed by God to be anointed king of Israel. God
richly blessed King David, and he had many wives and concubines.
However, his wealth and power did not satisfy the desires of his heart.
He wanted more.

Read the account of David's slide into sin in 2 Samuel 11. As you read, think about how David's idols led him to sin.

1. If anyone should have recognized the need to confess sin at several points in this account, one would have thought that David would have done so. Instead, he made several attempts to cover up his sin.
    *   What actions did he take to conceal his sins?
    *   How does Proverbs 28:13 address our attempts to cover up our sins?

2. In addition to concealing his sins, what other sins did David commit in this account?

3. What did David's sins reveal about the following idols?
    *   Improper desires for physical pleasure
    *   Pride and arrogance
    *   Love of money or material possessions
    *   Fear of man
    *   Good things that he wanted too much

4. What was David willing to sacrifice in order to serve his idols?

5. How is David's slide into these sins similar to our own struggle with sin and the idols of our hearts?

How can the idolatrous sinner be reconciled to God?

The sinner often needs help to recognize and admit sin. God sent the prophet Nathan to guide David to be reconciled to God. Read 2 Samuel 12:1-13.

6. David had blinded himself to the seriousness of his sins, and he thought that he had sufficiently hidden his sin from others. What was God's response to David's actions according to 2 Samuel 11:27 and also 2 Samuel 12:13?

7. How does David's experience with his own self-deception compare to what we do when we deny our sin?

8. Although King David attempted to cover up and deny his sin, the prophet Nathan helped David recognize his sin and confess to God. Reflecting on 2 Samuel 12:1-6, what did Nathan do that was so effective in convicting David of his sin?

9. How was King David reconciled to God (2 Samuel 12:13)?

Our sinful nature leads us to ignore our sin or try to cover it up. We desire to be righteous and to be judged by others as basically good people. One way to accomplish this is by denying that we have done anything sinful. However, God warns against the denial of our sin.

10. Read 1 John 1:8. Note how John defines "the truth" in John 14:6.
    • "The truth" is defined as _____.

11. Read 1 John 1:10. Note how John defines "his word" in John 1:1 and 14.
    • John 1:1 and 14. "The Word" is defined as

    _____.

12. As you think of John's definitions of "the truth" and "his word," what is the implication when we deny our sin in 1 John 1:8 and 10?

13. Those who claim to be without sin justify themselves. What did Jesus say about those who were self-righteous?
    • Matthew 9:10-13
    • Matthew 23:27-28

The self-righteous do not need the Savior. Those who deny their own sin deny their need for Jesus. They believe that their own good deeds make them righteous.

14. What do the Scriptures teach about us when we depend on our own good deeds for righteousness?
    - Isaiah 64:6-7
    - Luke 18:9-14

15. In the parable of the Pharisee and the tax collector, what led to righteousness for the tax collector?

16. What Good News is available for those who confess their sins before God?
    - Proverbs 28:13
    - 1 John 1:9

17. We cannot make ourselves righteous, and our sin separates us from God (Isaiah 59:2). Remembering that the wages of sin is death (Romans 6:23), how can we stand before God and not be condemned?
    - 2 Corinthians 5:21
    - Romans 1:16-17
    - Romans 8:1

Scripture teaches that we are poor, miserable sinners, unable to do anything on our own to earn favor with God. We come to the throne of God as beggars, with nothing to offer to atone for our sinful nature or sinful behaviors. Note how the hymn, "Rock of Ages, Cleft for Me," reflects our helpless condition:

> Nothing in my hand I bring;
> Simply to Thy cross I cling.
> Naked, come to Thee for dress;
> Helpless, look to Thee for grace;
> Foul, I to the fountain fly;
> Wash me, Savior, or I die.[2]

God has had mercy on us sinners, placing all of our sins upon His Son and giving us the righteousness of Jesus.

---

2 Augustus M. Toplady, 1740-78; "Rock of Ages, Cleft for Me," 3rd stanza, public domain.

Christ died for the sins of the whole world, but not all people will be saved. Read John 3:16-18.

18. Who will be saved from eternal damnation?

19. Who will not be saved?

Note how the *Augsburg Confession* defines repentance, including what happens as a result:

> Properly speaking, repentance consists of these two parts: one is contrition, that is, terror smiting the conscience with a knowledge of sin, and the other is faith, which is born of the Gospel, or of absolution, believes that sins are forgiven for Christ's sake, comforts the conscience, and delivers it from terror. Then good works, which are the fruits of repentance, are bound to follow.[3]

20. The first part of repentance is contrition. How does the above definition describe "contrition"? How is that meaning minimized in our culture?

21. What is the second part of repentance?

22. Martin Luther said, "The more you minimize sin, the more will grace decline in value."[4] Give an example that illustrates what Luther was saying.

23. What results from repentance?

Christ's forgiveness for our sins, including our idolatry, restores us in our relationship with God. We confess our faith when we confess our sins to God and believe in the Good News that for Jesus' sake we are forgiven.

Knowing that we are forgiven then enables us to do the good works that God plans for us to do. Notice how the Apostle Paul describes this in Ephesians 2:8-10.

---

3 The Augsburg Confession, Article XII.3-6 in Theodore G. Tappert, ed., *The Book of Concord: The Confessions of the Evangelical Lutheran Church* (Philadelphia: Fortress Press, 1959), 34-35.

4 *Luther's Works*, Volume 1 (St. Louis: CPH, 1958), 142.

Daily Confession

In Lesson 1, we reflected on the meaning of our Baptism including the following:

What does such baptizing with water indicate?

It indicates that the Old Adam in us should by daily contrition and repentance be drowned and die with all sins and evil desires, and that a new man should daily emerge and arise to live before God in righteousness and purity forever.

24. Why is daily contrition necessary for the child of God?

25. What does confession of sin indicate about our faith in Jesus?

26. Read 1 Peter 2:24. What specifically empowers us to live as God's people?

Living in Forgiveness

We are forgiven! But the temptations of our sinful flesh, the world, and the devil can lead us to doubt this truth. Our doubt is revealed:

- when we lose sight of whose we are through Baptism,
- when we forget what God has done for us in Christ,
- when we self-justify in order to make ourselves righteous.

27. According to 2 Peter 1:9, what is the cause of people not bearing good fruit?

28. Remembering that we are forgiven in Christ is the key to living as the children of God. Identify the means that God has given us to be assured of God's forgiveness.

- Corporate _____ _____

  _____

- Private _____ _____

  _____ with my pastor

- Confession and forgiveness with a _____ or

  _____ in Christ

- The _____ of God

- The _____ _____

- Remembering my _____

When guilt or doubts threaten to take away your joy in Christ's forgiveness, focus on God's assurance for you. Read these passages of Scripture aloud, inserting your name:

- "For our sake he made him to be sin who knew no sin, so that in him [Name] might become the righteousness of God" (2 Corinthians 5:21).
- "But now in Christ Jesus [Name] who once [was] far off [has] been brought near by the blood of Christ" (Ephesians 2:13).
- "As far as the east is from the west, so far does he remove [Name's] transgressions from [him/her]" (Psalm 103:12).

 ## Case Study

Kyle and Nicole were engaged to be married in three months. For several years, Kyle had been working as a production manager in a company that produced specialized components for the heavy equipment industry. Business was booming. His boss offered to promote him to plant manager if he would agree to do whatever the boss asked him to do. The promotion meant a raise plus large bonuses. Kyle quickly agreed, thinking that the increased income would be great for a new marriage. He didn't ask his boss what was meant by "do whatever the boss asked."

Two weeks into his new position, his boss asked him again about his commitment. Kyle affirmed his agreement, apprehensive of where this was leading. The boss told him that two of the plant employees were older (early 60's), and that meant that their seniority wages and health insurance were costing the company more expense than younger employees. In addition, they weren't as energetic as the younger guys on the team. So, Kyle needed to begin documenting everything these two guys did wrong so that Kyle could justify firing them in the next 45 days. His boss promised to give him a bonus equaling 1/3 of the savings in annual health insurance costs, which would amount to a few thousand dollars.

Kyle's heart sank. He respected both of the older workers, knowing that they were solid workers. Their families were dependent upon their incomes. Kyle feared it would be difficult for them at their ages to find new jobs that paid as well. He regretted his promise to "do whatever" just to get the promotion, and he resented his boss for setting him up.

Kyle began to document, even exaggerate, the severity of the two mens' mistakes. He raised his voice with them whenever they slipped up, letting them know they were being written up. Guilt started to overcome him as a Christian. Their mistakes were no worse than others' mistakes, including his own. He knew what he was doing was wrong – even evil. He was unable to sleep well at night. He became moody and snapped at Nicole for the smallest things. She asked him what was wrong, but Kyle was reluctant to tell her what was bugging him. In fact, he hadn't told anyone. He felt trapped and began to fall into a depression. Nicole wondered if her fiancé was having second thoughts about the wedding.

 ## Application Questions

These questions can apply to the above case study or to a current conflict from your personal life. For the case study, assume Kyle's role. For a conflict from your life, apply these questions to yourself, writing out your answers.

1. Which of the following idols are you guilty of in this situation? (Review the application questions at the end of Lesson 2 if you have not done so.)
    a. Improper desires for physical pleasure
    b. Pride and arrogance
    c. Love of money or material possessions
    d. Fear of man
    e. Good things that I want too much

2. Besides the individuals with whom you are in conflict, which others are being affected by your thoughts, words, or actions?

3. What is keeping you from confessing your sins against God before one of the following:
   - Your pastor?
   - A mature Christian with whom you are not related but whom you trust?
   - A mature Christian with whom you are related and who loves you?

   a. Pray that God will take away your fear of confessing before another person and give you courage.
   b. If you continue to struggle with your guilt and yet are reluctant to confess to someone who will proclaim God's forgiveness to you, seek out your pastor or a mature Christian for advice and encouragement.

4. Application of confession and hearing God's forgiveness proclaimed to you:
   - Make an appointment with your pastor or a mature Christian believer.

   - Explain that you desire to confess your sin to God before another person so that you might audibly hear God's forgiveness proclaimed to you by another Christian.
     ◦ If the person is not your pastor, ask for his or her commitment to keep what you confess confidential (pastors vow to keep private confession confidential).
     ◦ Tell the person that you have a simple form that will help guide you both.

   - When you meet, you may give some background of the situation if helpful for you. But such background is not necessary for the person hearing your confession.

   - Consider asking the person to use the form enclosed with this Bible study (*Proclaiming God's Forgiveness*). Using that form, you can confess your sins to God, and the person hearing your confession can proclaim God's forgiveness to you. If confessing to your pastor, he can also use a form for private absolution found in the hymnal or catechism.

- Your confession may be general or it may include specifics. God knows more about your sin than you do, and He does not need details in order for Him to forgive. However, if a specific sin is troubling you, confessing that particular sin aloud will help you to "own" your sin. More importantly, when God's forgiveness is proclaimed to you, it will help you to "own" the forgiveness, providing you with special comfort and assurance.

- Whether or not the form is used, be sure to request that the person hearing your confession specifically use Bible verses in proclaiming God's forgiveness (many are included in the form enclosed with this Bible study).

- Ask the person to pray for you.

Be Reconciled to Others

4: Confess to the Other Person

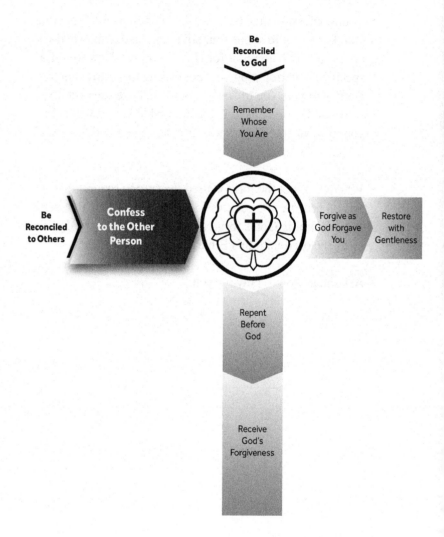

What does it mean to be reconciled to Others?
Matthew 5:23-24

4: Confess to the Other Person

How does my confession lead to reconciliation?

 Review from *Luther's Small Catechism*:
The Creed

As the head of the family should teach it in a simple way to his household

The First Article: Creation

I believe in God, the Father Almighty, Maker of heaven and earth.

What does this mean? I believe that God has made me and all creatures; that He has given me my body and soul, eyes, ears, and all my members, my reason and all my senses, and still takes care of them.

He also gives me clothing and shoes, food and drink, house and home, wife and children, land, animals, and all I have. He richly and daily provides me with all that I need to support this body and life.

He defends me against all danger and guards and protects me from all evil.

All this He does only out of fatherly, divine goodness and mercy, without any merit or worthiness in me. For all this it is my duty to thank and praise, serve and obey Him.

This is most certainly true.

The Second Article: Redemption

And in Jesus Christ, his only Son, our Lord, who was conceived by the Holy Spirit, born of the Virgin Mary, suffered under Pontius Pilate, was crucified, died and was buried. He descended into hell. The third day He rose again from the dead. He ascended into heaven and sits at the right hand of God, the Father Almighty. From thence He will come to judge the living and the dead.

What does this mean? I believe that Jesus Christ, true God, begotten of the Father from eternity, and also true man, born of the Virgin Mary, is my Lord,

who has redeemed me, a lost and condemned person, purchased and won me from all sins, from death, and from the power of the devil; not with gold or silver, but with His holy, precious blood and with His innocent suffering and death,

that I may be His own and live under Him in His kingdom and serve Him in everlasting righteousness, innocence, and blessedness,

just as He is risen from the dead, lives and reigns to all eternity.

This is most certainly true.

The Third Article: Sanctification

I believe in the Holy Spirit, the holy Christian church, the communion of saints, the forgiveness of sins, the resurrection of the body, and the life everlasting. Amen.

What does this mean? I believe that I cannot by my own reason or strength believe in Jesus Christ, my Lord, or come to Him; but the Holy Spirit has called me by the Gospel, enlightened me with his gifts, sanctified and kept me in the true faith.

In the same way He calls, gathers, enlightens, and sanctifies the whole Christian church on earth, and keeps it with Jesus Christ in the one true faith.

In this Christian church He daily and richly forgives all my sins and the sins of all believers.

On the Last Day He will raise me and all the dead, and give eternal life to me and all believers in Christ.

This is most certainly true.

How do my sins affect others?

When we sin against God, we usually sin against others. These offenses harm our relationships with those we hurt. Our sins also affect others, directly and indirectly. How we treat one another affects our witness to Christ and our faith in the forgiveness of sins.

Consider James, a teenage son who failed to return home with the car at the time required by his mother. He got so caught up in his personal activities with friends that he neglected to watch the time, and his cell phone was dead because he forgot to charge it. He arrived home an hour late. His mother needed the car to pick up her younger daughter Amy from the dentist's office. This resulted in the dentist being late for one of his commitments as he had to wait at his office for Amy to be picked up. The dentist expressed his anger to Amy's mother on the phone.

When James arrived home late, he sinned against God by disobeying and dishonoring his mother (4th Commandment) and breaking his word (8th Commandment). These were also sins against the 1st Commandment (James essentially made himself a "god," living to please his own desires).

1. How might James' sins against God's commands harm his relationship with his mother?

2. Besides his mother, who else is affected by James' actions?

When James arrived late, his mother unleashed her anger against him. She yelled at him, calling him names, and told him he can no longer use the car – he was grounded. James yelled back at his mother, reminding her that she was 30 minutes late to pick him up after school one time and over an hour late after basketball games twice in the last week. That meant that James had less time to do homework, and his grades suffered as a result. He called her a bad name and shouted, "Now *you* know what it feels like!"

Although James sinned by coming home late and deserves

consequences for his actions, both James and his mother sinned against one another in their confrontation.

3. How do the following Scripture passages apply to James' mother in her response to her son's sin?
   - Galatians 6:1-2
   - Ephesians 6:4
   - James 3:1

4. Instead of confessing his sin, how did James justify himself?

5. In Lesson 3, we learned what happens when we justify ourselves. Apply 1 John 1:8 & 10 to James in his self-justification.

6. If you were a trusted friend of James and heard his story, how would you advise James as to what he should have done as a child of God when he was confronted by his mother?

7. No matter how his mother responded to his sin, what comfort can you provide James as he recognizes his faults in this situation?
   - Proverbs 28:13
   - 1 John 1:9
   - 1 Peter 2:24

8. What would you encourage James to do now?

9. If you were a trusted friend of James' mother and heard about the confrontation from her, how could the following verses provide counsel for her?
   - James 5:16
   - Matthew 5:23-24
   - 1 Peter 2:24

10. What other verses would apply to either James or his mother?

What are the dangers of anger?

While we may not show as much outward anger or disrespect as James and his mother, our inner reactions to conflict can be just as sinful in God's eyes. Consider the following possibilities. Reflect on how Ephesians 4:29-32 might apply.

11. We may lose our temper and say hurtful things that bring harm and not healing.
    • Ephesians 4:29

12. Angry words do not only hurt the ones to whom we declare them. Who else is affected?
    • Ephesians 4:30

13. Instead of talking with one another to gently restore, we may avoid talking all together. But in our hearts, resentment or grudges can build up.
    • Ephesians 4:31

14. Instead of anger and bitterness, our God shows us another way.
    • Ephesians 4:32

There are times when anger may be an appropriate response. In fact, people often speak of "righteous anger." Certainly, our God disapproves of sinful activity and expresses His anger at sinful behavior. But God also knows how to perfectly control His anger.

15. What can we learn about God and the use of anger from the following passages?
    • Psalm 30:4-5
    • Psalm 103:8-13

As sinful beings, we may lose sight of how long our anger should last. Scripture warns against misusing anger.

16. According to Ephesians 4:26-27, how long should we allow our anger to last? What are the consequences of not dealing with our anger in a timely fashion?

When we lose our temper, we might justify it. "You made me so angry!" is actually a form of self-justification. In truth, no one can make me angry but me.

17. What are other dangers of our anger?
   • Proverbs 14:29
   • Proverbs 15:1
   • Proverbs 22:24-25
   • James 1:20

How does confession or denial reflect my confession of faith?

In Lesson 3, we saw how a denial of sin is a denial of our need for Christ. Instead of depending on Christ and His forgiveness, we justify ourselves.

However, when we confess our sins, trusting in God's forgiveness of sins, we confess our faith in Christ. 1 John 1:9 teaches, "If we confess our sins, he is faithful and just to forgive us our sins and to cleanse us from all unrighteousness."

The Greek word translated "confess" (ὁμολογῶμεν – homologōmen) means "say the same thing." When we confess our sins, we say the same thing that God says – we are sinful and deserve nothing but God's wrath and punishment (e.g., Romans 6:23a). Notice how the Apostle Paul uses the same term "confess" in Romans 10:9-10.

When we *confess* our faith in the words of the Apostles' Creed, we say the same thing that God says in His Word – He created me, He redeemed me, and He sanctifies me.

In Luther's explanation to the Third Article, we *confess* that the Holy Spirit "sanctifies the whole Christian church on earth." And in this Christian Church, God "daily and richly forgives all my sins and the sins of all believers."

When we *confess* our sins, we *confess* our faith in Christ. We acknowledge that we need a Savior and we trust in His forgiveness. As we confess in the Apostles' Creed, our confession of sin is a demonstration that we believe our faith in the forgiveness of sins.

But when we deny our sin, or whenever we self-justify, we profess a different confession of faith.

> 18. When we fail to confess our sin, whom are we trusting (and in whom are we placing our faith) for justification? What does this imply about our profession of faith?

Who is responsible for taking the first step?

In most disputes, each party contributes to the conflict. Even if one initiates the conflict, the other person's reaction or failure to act in a godly way fuels the discord.

> 19. According to God's Word, who is responsible for taking the initiative in reconciliation?
> - Matthew 5:23-24
> - Matthew 18:15
> - Romans 12:18

Confessing to Others

> 20. What leads to healing in James 5:16?

In our culture, we are conditioned to "apologize" when we do something wrong. We often speak about apologizing to one another.

However, the word "apologize" is a poor substitute for the word "confess." It can mean "express regret for doing something wrong." But it can also mean "make a defense." (For example, the *Apology to the Augsburg Confession* is not a statement of regret but rather a defense.)

Note that the Bible does not use the word "apologize" when speaking about confessing wrongs (e.g., see Proverbs 28:13; 1 John 1:9; James 5:16).

Because unbelievers do not know what it means to confess to God and be forgiven, the unbelieving world uses the word "apologize." But for the Christian, "confess" is a biblical term that better reflects godly contrition.

21. Likewise, the words "I'm sorry" have multiple meanings. What are some of the meanings of the word "I'm sorry?"

Guidelines for Confession

Expressing godly sorrow in confession reflects true contrition – it is a fruit of repentance. However, we are so accustomed to self-justifying that our words often serve to avoid taking responsibility for our sin. Instead, our words seek to blame others or explain away our guilt.

22. What are the two kinds of sorrow or grief identified in 2 Corinthians 7:10?

23. How would you distinguish the two kinds of sorrow or grief?

24. What are some of the ways that an "apology" can fail to express godly sorrow?

25. To express godly sorrow in our confession, consider the following "Guidelines for Confession":

   • Go as a _____.
     ◦ Matthew 5:23-24
     ◦ Luke 15:19
     ◦ Luke 18:13-14
     ◦ James 5:16

   Jesus' words are clear: Go! Approach those you have sinned against and confess to them. Remember that there is nothing you can do to earn their favor or their forgiveness. You humble yourself as a beggar with nothing to bring, asking for their undeserved mercy. Be sure to go to all those who have been affected – not just the person with whom you are directly in conflict.

- _____ your sin.
  - Numbers 5:5-7
  - Psalm 32:3-5
  - Psalm 51:3-4

  Make no excuses. Don't blame others. Avoid language that minimizes your confession or shifts blame (e.g., words like *if* or *but*). For example, consider saying "I was wrong" rather than the normal "I'm sorry," which can mean something other than "I was wrong."

- Identify your sins according to _____ _____.
  Indicate which commandments or portions of Scripture you have violated. You may identify specific thoughts, words, or actions. Sins may include things you have not done (sins of omission). You may also state that your sins against the other person were also sins against God (note Psalm 51:4 and the prodigal son's confession to his father in Luke 15:18).
  - Sinful thoughts – Ecclesiastes 2:1-3; Matthew 15:19; Luke 6:45
  - Sinful words – Exodus 20:16; Proverbs 11:13; Ephesians 4:29
  - Sinful actions – Exodus 20:12-17; Matthew 7:12; Galatians 5:19-21
  - Sins of omission, such as failing to love as Christ commands – 1 Corinthians 13:4-7

- Express _____ _____ _____
  your sin has caused.
  "My sin hurt you by..." or "I am sorry for how my actions hurt you when..."
  - Luke 15:21

  If you are unsure how your behavior was hurtful, ask! ("How have my actions hurt you?")

- Commit to _____ _____ _____
  with God's help.
  "With God's help, I will not do this again."
  - Psalm 51:10-12

> ○ Matthew 3:8
> ○ Luke 19:8
> ○ Romans 6:21-22
> ○ Ephesians 4:22-24

- Be willing to _____ _____

  _____.

  With God's forgiveness, the consequences of eternal death
  have been removed. However, even with forgiveness,
  there may be earthly consequences. Your recognition of
  consequences demonstrates fruit of repentance and helps
  communicate godly sorrow. Note that the consequences may
  include restitution to restore the person harmed by the sin
  (such as paying for damage to another's property or paying for
  medical expenses).
  > ○ Numbers 5:5-7
  > ○ Luke 15:19
  > ○ Luke 19:8

- Ask for _____.

  "I ask for your forgiveness." Don't demand it, but ask as a
  beggar seeking mercy. With God, forgiveness is instantaneous,
  constant, and always available. But with people, it often is
  a process and takes time. Remember that even a perfect
  confession does not deserve forgiveness. Forgiveness is a gift
  and cannot be earned, bought, or deserved.
  > ○ Genesis 50:17
  > ○ Psalm 32:5
  > ○ Matthew 5:23-24
  > ○ Luke 18:13

- Trust in _____

  _____.

  Whether or not the other person forgives you, remember that
  you are forgiven in Christ based on the promises of Holy
  Scripture.
  > ○ Psalm 103:8-13

- Colossians 1:13-14
- "In him we have redemption through his blood, the forgiveness of our trespasses, according to the riches of his grace, which he lavished upon us, in all wisdom and insight making known to us the mystery of his will, according to his purpose, which he set forth in Christ as a plan for the fullness of time, to unite all things in him, things in heaven and things on earth." (Ephesians 1:7-10)

While not every one of the above guidelines is necessary for a godly confession, these can help you take full responsibility for your part in a conflict and avoid denying your sin or blame-shifting.

Review the following confession to God from the Divine Service.

> Most merciful God, we confess that we are by nature sinful and unclean. We have sinned against You in thought, word, and deed, by what we have done and by what we have left undone. We have not loved You with our whole heart; we have not loved our neighbors as ourselves. We justly deserve Your present and eternal punishment. For the sake of Your Son, Jesus Christ, have mercy on us. Forgive us, renew us, and lead us, so that we may delight in Your will and walk in Your ways to the glory of Your holy name. Amen.[5]

26. Identify which of the Guidelines for Confession are included in the corporate confession above.

27. What if one of the parties is not a Christian? Should that change the way you confess?

 ## Case Study

As an alternative to reading the following Case Study, utilize the skit "You Wrecked My Car!" Or, watch the video "Father & Son 1" from the DVD Responding to Sexual Temptation in a High Tech Society. *You can order both the skit and DVD from www.hisaor.org in the bookstore.*

---

5 "Divine Service Setting One." Lutheran Service Book. Saint Louis, MO: Concordia Publishing House, 2006. 151. Print.

Matt is a 17-year-old with his new driving license. His parents have a house rule that Matt is not allowed to drive without first gaining permission from them. One evening while Matt's parents were gone, Matt's friend Jake called. Jake had just broken up with his girlfriend and was upset. Without contacting his parents, Matt immediately went out of the house, taking his father's Jeep. When backing the Jeep out of the driveway, Matt backed into a retaining wall and broke a taillight. But he was in such a hurry that he didn't notice. He then picked up Jake and drove around so that they could talk. He returned home before his parents and parked the Jeep back in the driveway.

When his parents came home, his father saw the damaged taillight and came into the house to confront his son. Matt denied taking the Jeep, and Matt's dad became angry, yelling and accusing him. Matt responded in anger, denying his actions and showing disrespect for his father. Without resolving the matter, Matt walked out on his father muttering, "Whatever!"

If using the skit or video, save Scene 2 (skit) or "Father & Son 2" (video) for Lesson 6.

 Application Questions

These questions can apply to the above case study or to a current conflict from your personal life. For the case study, assume either Matt's or his father's role. For a conflict from your life, apply these questions to yourself, writing out your answers.

1. If you could go back in time and do anything differently in your encounter with the other person, what would that be? Reflecting on your answer, what have you failed to do as a child of God?

2. Consider whether you have any bitterness against the other person. Read Ephesians 4:26-27. How long have you been angry? How has your bitterness become a foothold for the devil?

3. Reflect on your words in your conflict with the other person.

Compare them to Ephesians 4:29-32. What words have you spoken to the other person that were not helpful for building up?

4. Think about others you have talked to about this situation. Comparing your speech to Luther's explanation to the 8th Commandment, how have you sinned? (Note especially the *pro-active* requirements of this Commandment in Luther's explanation below.)

What does this mean? We should fear and love God so that we do not tell lies about our neighbor, betray him, slander him, or hurt his reputation, but *defend him, speak well of him, and explain everything in the kindest way* (emphasis added).

5. Read Philippians 2:14-15. Whether or not you talked to someone else, have you grumbled or complained about the other person?

6. What behaviors did you exhibit that failed to follow God's commands?

7. Compare your thoughts, words, and actions to what the Bible describes in 1 Corinthians 13:4-7. How have you failed to love the other people involved?

8. Prepare to express your confession to the other person. Use the Guidelines for Confession to write out the words you could use.
   • Go as a beggar.
   • Own your sin.
   • Identify your sins according to God's Word.
   • Express sorrow for hurt your sin has caused.
   • Commit to changing your behavior with God's help.
   • Be willing to bear the consequences.
   • Ask for forgiveness.
   • Trust in Christ's forgiveness.

9. Write a prayer for God's help in confessing to the other person.

Be Reconciled to Others

5: Forgive as God Forgave You

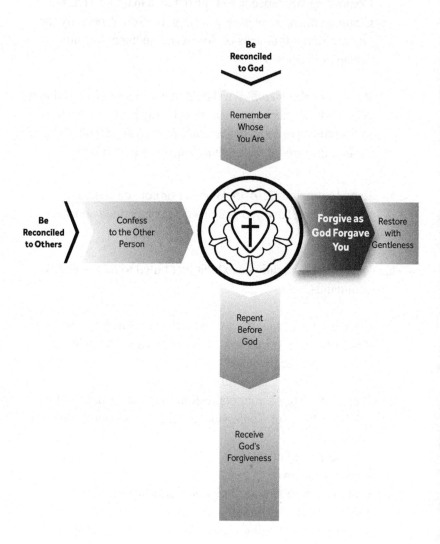

What does it mean to be reconciled to Others?
Matthew 5:23-24

5: Forgive as God Forgave You

How does forgiving and resolving lead to reconciliation?

 Review from *Luther's Small Catechism:*
The Lord's Prayer

As the head of the family should teach it in a simple way to his household

> Our Father who art in heaven, hallowed be Thy name, Thy kingdom come, Thy will be done on earth as it is in heaven. Give us this day our daily bread; and forgive us our trespasses as we forgive those who trespass against us; and lead us not into temptation, but deliver us from evil. For Thine is the kingdom and the power and the glory forever and ever. Amen.

The Introduction
Our Father who art in heaven.

> *What does this mean?* With these words God tenderly invites us to believe that He is our true Father and that we are His true children, so that with all boldness and confidence we may ask Him as dear children ask their father.

The First Petition
Hallowed be Thy name.

> *What does this mean?* God's name is certainly holy in itself, but we pray in this petition that it may be kept holy among us also.

> *How is God's name kept holy?* God's name is kept holy when the Word of God is taught in its truth and purity, and we, as the children of God, also lead holy lives according to it. Help us to do this, dear Father in heaven! But anyone who teaches

or lives contrary to God's Word profanes the name of God among us. Protect us from this, heavenly Father!

The Second Petition

Thy kingdom come.

> *What does this mean?* The kingdom of God certainly comes by itself without our prayer, but we pray in this petition that it may come to us also.
>
> *How does God's kingdom come?* God's kingdom comes when our heavenly Father gives us His Holy Spirit, so that by His grace we believe His holy Word and lead godly lives here in time and there in eternity.

The Third Petition

Thy will be done on earth as it is in heaven.

> *What does this mean?* The good and gracious will of God is done even without our prayer, but we pray in this petition that it may be done among us also.
>
> *How is God's will done?* God's will is done when He breaks and hinders every evil plan and purpose of the devil, the world, and our sinful nature, which do not want us to hallow God's name or let His kingdom come;
>
> and when He strengthens and keeps us firm in his Word and faith until we die.
>
> This is His good and gracious will.

The Fourth Petition

Give us this day our daily bread.

> *What does this mean?* God certainly gives daily bread to everyone without our prayers, even to all evil people, but we pray in this petition that God would lead us to realize this and to receive our daily bread with thanksgiving.
>
> *What is meant by daily bread?* Daily bread includes

everything that has to do with the support and needs of the body, such as food, drink, clothing, shoes, house, home, land, animals, money, goods, a devout husband or wife, devout children, devout workers, devout and faithful rulers, good government, good weather, peace, health, self-control, good reputation, good friends, faithful neighbors, and the like.

The Fifth Petition

And forgive us our trespasses as we forgive those who trespass against us.

> *What does this mean?* We pray in this petition that our Father in heaven would not look at our sins, or deny our prayer because of them. We are neither worthy of the things for which we pray, nor have we deserved them, but we ask that He would give them all to us by grace, for we daily sin much and surely deserve nothing but punishment. So we too will sincerely forgive and gladly do good to those who sin against us.

The Sixth Petition

And lead us not into temptation.

> *What does this mean?* God tempts no one. We pray in this petition that God would guard and keep us so that the devil, the world, and our sinful nature may not deceive us or mislead us into false belief, despair, and other great shame and vice. Although we are attacked by these things, we pray that we may finally overcome them and win the victory.

The Seventh Petition

But deliver us from evil.

> *What does this mean?* We pray in this petition, in summary, that our Father in heaven would rescue us from every evil of body and soul, possessions and reputation, and finally, when our last hour comes, give us a blessed end, and graciously take us from this valley of sorrow to Himself in heaven.

What are some false substitutes for forgiving?

Paul instructs us believers: "Put on then, as God's chosen ones, holy and beloved, compassionate hearts, kindness, humility, meekness, and patience, bearing with one another and, if one has a complaint against another, forgiving each other; as the Lord has forgiven you, so you also must forgive" (Colossians 3:12-13).

"Forgiving as the Lord has forgiven you" is often misunderstood, even among God's elect. Our society has conditioned us to use false substitutes for the biblical language, "I forgive you as Christ has forgiven me."

1. Identify what is biblically false or weak in the following:
    * Excusing: Phrases such as *That's okay, No problem, or Don't worry about it*
      ◦ Isaiah 59:2
      ◦ Romans 6:23a
      ◦ James 2:10

    * Punishing: *You deserve my judgment and condemnation*
      ◦ Luke 6:36-37
      ◦ Romans 2:1
      ◦ James 4:11-12

    * Earning: *I won't forgive you until you deserve it or earn it*
      ◦ Romans 6:23b
      ◦ Romans 5:15
      ◦ Ephesians 2:8-9

    * Recalling: *I will never let you forget what you did!*
      ◦ Jeremiah 31:34
      ◦ Psalm 103:8-10
      ◦ 2 Corinthians 5:17, 21

How does God forgive me?

We deserve God's full wrath and punishment, including eternal death. Yet God forgives us so completely that we are considered holy – fully righteous in the sight of God.

2. Note how God forgives me:
   - My sins are not excused; God's justice required

     _____.
     - ◦ Hebrews 9:22
     - ◦ 1 John 1:7
   - My sins needed to be punished: Christ _____ the full price for my sins.
     - ◦ Isaiah 53:5-6
     - ◦ John 19:30
   - My forgiveness is _____ _____ upon my works.
     - ◦ Romans 6:23b
     - ◦ Ephesians 2:8-10
   - My past sins will not be _____ _____ and used against me.
     - ◦ Jeremiah 31:34
     - ◦ 1 Corinthians 6:11
   - My sins do not _____ me.
     - ◦ John 3:17
     - ◦ Romans 8:1
   - My sins have been washed clean – I am covered by Christ's

     _____.
     - ◦ Romans 3:21-22
     - ◦ 2 Corinthians 5:21

How can I forgive as the Lord forgives me?

In the Fifth Petition of the Lord's Prayer, we pray, "Forgive us our trespasses as we forgive those who trespass against us."

How often have we prayed those words and yet held bitterness or grudges against someone else?

3.   When teaching His disciples to pray this prayer, what warning did Jesus give for this petition in Matthew 6:14-15?

4.   What did Jesus mean? Does our heavenly Father only forgive us *if and when* we forgive those who have sinned against?

5.   Why is it so difficult to forgive as God has forgiven us?

When we forgive others, we give witness to our faith in Christ and what He has done and is doing for us. When I forgive as God has forgiven me, I am living my confession of faith.

6.   What do I demonstrate in forgiving others?

  • That I believe in my own _____ _____

      _____.
      ◦ Acts 10:43
      ◦ Ephesians 1:7-12
      ◦ Colossians 3:12-13

  • That I believe that Jesus died for the sins of _____

      _____, including those who have sinned
      against me.
      ◦ Luke 23:34, 42-43
      ◦ John 3:16
      ◦ Romans 3:23-26

  • That I remember that I am a forgiven _____

      _____ _____, saved by His grace.
      ◦ John 1:12-13
      ◦ 1 John 3:1
      ◦ Ephesians 1:7

  • That I am a _____ _____ _____ who

      loves others as God _____ _____.
      ◦ John 13:34-35

- ○ 1 John 4:10-12
- ○ 1 Peter 4:8

7. What does it demonstrate when we fail to forgive others as God has forgiven us?
   - Matthew 18:21-35
   - 2 Peter 1:9
   - Colossians 3:12-13

Paul writes in Ephesians 4:32: "Be kind to one another, tenderhearted, forgiving one another, as God in Christ forgave you." Forgiving others as God has forgiven us is *impossible* – on our own strength. Yet our God calls us to do to others as He has done for us.

8. What power or abilities does God promise to give His children?
   - Ephesians 3:14-21
   - 1 Peter 2:24
   - Philippians 4:13

Does forgiveness remove consequences?

In a congregation where a church treasurer embezzled from church funds, the congregation was polarized on how to respond. Some said, "We must not show any mercy. He deserves to go to jail and rot!" Others said, "Wait, aren't we Christians? We're supposed to forgive and forget!"

9. Why does neither of these viewpoints present a biblical perspective?

Does forgiveness relieve consequences? Before you answer too quickly, let's review what Scripture teaches.

10. What consequence does forgiveness always relieve?
    - Romans 6:23
    - Romans 8:1

Can there be both forgiveness and earthy consequences? Consider the following:

11. Moses sinned against God by striking the rock at Meribah-kadesh rather than speaking to it as God commanded (Numbers 20:10-13). What was the earthly consequence for his sin?
    • Deuteronomy 32:48-52

12. What is the New Testament evidence that Moses was forgiven by God?
    • Mark 9:2-4

13. In Lesson 3, we reviewed the many ways in which King David sinned in his affair with Bathsheba and his execution of Uriah.
    • What is the evidence that David was forgiven by God?
      ◦ 2 Samuel 12:13
    • What were the earthly consequences for David's sin?
      ◦ 2 Samuel 12:10-12, 14

Note that the Bible teaches that forgiveness does not necessarily remove the earthly consequences. Nevertheless, our Lord often shows great mercy, withholding the consequences. An example is given in the parable of the prodigal son (Luke 15:11-32) in which the father showed great mercy to his repentant son.

14. When considering how to balance mercy with consequences, consider the purposes of consequences:
    • Consequences may be necessary to provide

      _____.
      ◦ Numbers 5:5-7
      ◦ Luke 19:8

    • Consequences may be a form of _____ for teaching the sinner.
      ◦ Proverbs 3:11-12
      ◦ Hebrews 12:11

- Consequences provide others an _____ or

  _____.
  - 1 Corinthians 5:6-7
  - Acts 5:5

- Consequences may protect a sinner from further

  _____.
  - Matthew 6:13
  - 1 Thessalonians 4:3-8; 5:22

Thus, it is important to consider the purposes and benefits of consequences when balancing mercy and consequences.

When should I forgive?

Jesus' disciples struggled with forgiveness.

15. What was the question that they asked Jesus regarding forgiveness?
    - Matthew 18:21-22

16. According to Jesus, what is the limited number of times we should forgive?

If we are to forgive as God forgave us, consider first how God forgives us.

17. When did or does God forgive me?
    - Romans 5:8
    - 1 John 1:9
    - Matthew 26:26-28
    - Acts 22:16
    - 1 Peter 2:24
    - Genesis 3:15
    - Ephesians 1:4

If God forgives me at these times, that means that He forgave me before I was born, which is before I knew I was a sinner, before I knew what Jesus did for me, and before I could repent.

18. If Jesus died for the sins of the whole world (John 3:16), and if His forgiveness was accomplished before we were born, then why is not everyone going to heaven?
    • John 3:18

Based on these questions, we can understand the relationship between repentance and forgiveness.

The *granting of forgiveness* is *not* dependent upon repentance.
    • God's forgiveness for us was not conditional on our repentance – He forgave us even while we were dead in our sins (Luke 23:34; Romans 5:6-10; Ephesians 2:1-5).

But the *receiving of forgiveness* is dependent upon repentance and faith.
    • We receive the benefit of God's forgiveness as we "repent and believe in Jesus" (John 3:16-18; Acts 3:19-20; Mark 1:15).

So, when should I forgive someone who has sinned against me? We are called to forgive others as God through Christ forgave us. That means we have the opportunity to grant forgiveness before the other person repents, even before we talk to him or her. However, the person who has sinned against us will not benefit from that forgiveness unless he repents and believes that the gift is his.

How does forgiveness relate to reconciliation?

Granting forgiveness is possible without repentance and confession. But repentance is needed for complete reconciliation (restoration of the relationship) to occur.

With this in mind, the purpose of restoring gently (confronting another about his sin) becomes even clearer.

We don't confront the other person so that she will repent in order to *earn* or *deserve* our forgiveness. You can *never* earn or deserve forgiveness – it is a free gift (Ephesians 2:8-9).

19. Then why do we confront another about his sin?
    - Mark 1:15
    - James 5:19-20

What does forgiving others in this way require?

20. What did the disciples realize is necessary to forgive someone repeatedly, even if they repent?
    - Luke 17:3-5

Jesus' disciples recognized that it takes great faith to forgive someone who sins against you repeatedly, even if they repent. Yet God does just that for us. Every day.

How can I resolve the material issues that divide us?

In Lesson 1, we noted the difference between *conflict resolution* and *reconciliation*.

In *conflict resolution*, we address the *material* or *substantive* issues of the conflict. We identify the problems to be solved and negotiate with the other person to resolve them.

In *reconciliation*, we seek to restore the relationship by addressing the relational or personal issues of the conflict. Relational issues are reconciled through confession and forgiveness.

Most of this Bible study has focused on *reconciliation*, which most people find is more difficult than *conflict resolution*.

Resolving the material issues is also necessary when addressing conflict.

21. What instruction does Scripture give when we need to resolve material issues?
   - Proverbs 16:1-3
   - Philippians 4:5-6
   - Matthew 22:39
   - Philippians 2:3-5
   - Philippians 2:14
   - Proverbs 12:15

22. What final instruction does Paul give the congregation at Philippi regarding the conflict between Euodia and Syntyche?
   - Philippians 4:8-9

 # Case Study

Amber, Nicole, and Kaitlyn shared everything. They played together on the college volleyball team. Between classes and practice, they always could be found together. The girls loved skiing in the winter and running in the warmer months. After college, each found employment in the same city where they attended church together. Nicole married first, then Amber. Kaitlyn remained single. But their friendship continued to flourish.

That is, until one day …

Amber and Kaitlyn exchanged some texts where Kaitlyn complained about Nicole. Kaitlyn thought that Nicole was acting arrogant because she married first, and Kaitlyn felt like Nicole was putting her down for not having a boyfriend. Amber defended Nicole and wrote some curt responses to Kaitlyn, who wrote back with hurtful words. Amber forwarded the whole exchange to Nicole. Nicole and Amber exchanged a flurry of texts in which they grumbled about all of Kaitlyn's idiosyncrasies and how she must be jealous of them. It didn't take long before Kaitlyn learned about the other two "ganging up" on her. She responded with angry texts to both of these friends. Before long, they were posting negative things about each other on Facebook and "unfriending" each other.

Once inseparable, Amber and Nicole now avoided Kaitlyn. It wasn't difficult to steer clear of one another, except at church. So they separately concluded that the best way not to see one another was to stop going to worship.

 ## Application Questions

These questions can apply to the above case study or to a current conflict from your personal life. For the case study, assume any of the three women's roles. For a conflict from your life, apply these questions to yourself, writing out your answers.

1. What has caused the hurt in your relationship:
    - For you personally?
    - For someone else you care about?
    - For the person who hurt you and others you care about?

2. How has your relationship with the other person changed?

3. What grieves you the most about what has happened?

4. What is keeping you from forgiving the other person?

5. How has your strained or broken relationship affected:
    - Your attitude toward the other person?
    - Your attitude toward yourself?
    - Your attitude toward others?
    - Your relationship with God?

6. What are some of the consequences of your unforgiveness?

7. You know that our heavenly Father commands that we forgive others as He forgives us. List at least ten sins from your life that God has forgiven through Christ.
    - Does God offer forgiveness to you for your bitterness and unforgiveness?
    - Reviewing this lesson, what Scripture passages give you comfort and assurance of God's forgiveness for all your sins?

8. Has Christ died for the sins of the person who hurt you or others you care about?
   • Reviewing this lesson, identify Scripture passages that support your answer.

9. For which sins of people did Christ not die?

10. Reflecting back on this lesson, what Scripture passages promise God's strength to forgive as He has forgiven you?

11. Write a prayer to God. You might include:
   • Confessing your sins of unforgiveness, bitterness, grudges, hatred, or anger that you may have in your heart.
   • Thanking Him for the forgiveness of all your sins.
   • Seeking His help to forgive as He has forgiven you.
   • Asking God to bless the person who has wronged you.
   • Praying that God reconciles your relationship with the other person.

Be Reconciled to Others

6: Restore with Gentleness

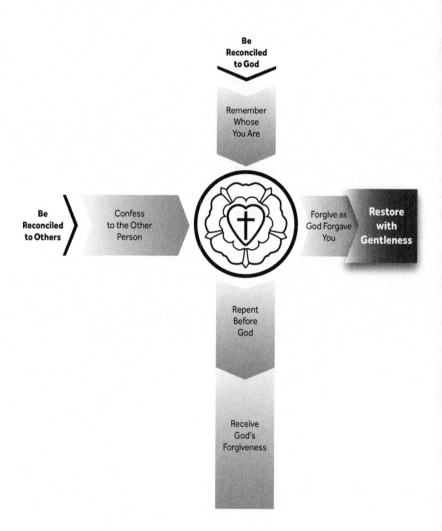

What does it mean to be reconciled to Others?

Matthew 5:23-24

6: Restore with Gentleness

How does restoring others lead to reconciliation?

 Review from *Luther's Small Catechism*:
The Sacrament of the Altar

As the head of the family should teach it in a simple way to his household

What is the Sacrament of the Altar?

It is the true body and blood of our Lord Jesus Christ under the bread and wine, instituted by Christ Himself for us Christians to eat and to drink.

Where is this written?

The holy Evangelists Matthew, Mark, Luke, and St. Paul write:

Our Lord Jesus Christ, on the night when He was betrayed, took bread, and when He had given thanks, He broke it and gave it to the disciples and said: "Take, eat; this is My body, which is given for you. This do in remembrance of Me."

In the same way also He took the cup after supper, and when He had given thanks, He gave it to them, saying, "Drink of it, all of you; this cup is the new testament in My blood, which is shed for you for the forgiveness of sins. This do, as often as you drink it, in remembrance of Me."

What is the benefit of this eating and drinking?

These words, "Given and shed for you for the forgiveness of sins," show us that in the Sacrament forgiveness of sins, life, and salvation are given us through these words. For where there is forgiveness of sins, there is also life and salvation.

How can bodily eating and drinking do such great things?

Certainly not just eating and drinking do these things, but the words written here: "Given and shed for you for the forgiveness of sins." These words, along with the bodily eating and drinking, are the main thing in the Sacrament. Whoever believes these words has exactly what they say: "forgiveness of sins."

Who receives this sacrament worthily?

Fasting and bodily preparation are certainly fine outward training. But that person is truly worthy and well prepared who has faith in these words: "Given and shed for you for the forgiveness of sins."

But anyone who does not believe these words or doubts them is unworthy and unprepared, for the words "for you" require all hearts to believe.

How does a person's sin harm relationships?

Our behavior affects others around us, directly and indirectly. When someone is ensnared by his sins, he hurts his relationship with others and gives a negative witness to anyone watching.

1. How does a person's sin harm his relationship with God?
   - Isaiah 59:2
   - Romans 8:7-8
   - James 1:14-15

2. How does unresolved conflict among Christians harm the church in which they belong?
   - 1 Corinthians 1:10-11; 3:1-4; 10:16-17
   - Galatians 5:13-15
   - Philippians 4:2-3

3. How do unreconciled relationships affect our witness to others?
   - John 13:34-35
   - 1 Corinthians 6:4-8
   - 1 Peter 2:12

4. Reflecting on the Bible passages from the three questions above, what difference does it make when people within the

same church remain unreconciled and yet commune at the same table?

In one of the collects following communion, we pray:

> We give thanks to You, almighty God, that You have refreshed us through this salutary gift, and we implore You that of Your mercy You would strengthen us through the same in faith toward You and in fervent love toward one another; through Jesus Christ, Your Son, our Lord, who lives and reigns with You and the Holy Spirit, one God, now and forever. Amen.[6]

5. How does the Lord's Supper strengthen believers to move in fervent love toward one another, including those within the same church who remain in conflict?
   - Matthew 26:26-28
   - 1 Corinthians 11:26 and 1 Peter 2:24
   - Philippians 4:13
   - 2 Corinthians 5:14-15

We are usually unaware of the number of people that are impacted by our strained relationships. As noted above, the body of Christ and our corporate witness can be affected. Thus, the Bible teaches that when two of the saints are entangled in conflict, others in the church need to help.

What does it mean to restore?

St. Paul addresses us through his letter to the Galatians: "Brothers, if anyone is caught in any transgression, you who are spiritual should restore him in a spirit of gentleness. Keep watch on yourself, lest you too be tempted. Bear one another's burdens, and so fulfill the law of Christ." (Galatians 6:1-2)

Helping one who is caught in sin often includes someone with whom we find ourselves in conflict.

6. Using the words from the above Scripture, who is the one that needs to be restored?

---

6 "Divine Service, Setting One," *Lutheran Service Book*, St. Louis: Concordia Publishing House, 2006. 166.

7. In the text above, who is the one that is called to restore?

8. Other passages also teach us to help others who need restoration. In the following texts, who is the one that needs to be restored? Who is called to restore?
   - Matthew 18:15
   - Philippians 4:2-3
   - James 5:19-20

The word translated "caught" in Galatians 6:1 can have different meanings in English. The original Greek word that is translated "caught" does not have the sense of "Aha! I caught you in the act!" Rather, "caught" means one who is entangled with sin. The Greek word in this text was also used when referring to a fish that was caught in a net or to an animal that is ensnared in a trap.

9. What is the danger of freeing an animal ensnared in a trap?

10. How might that relate to restoring a brother ensnared in a sin?

The word translated "restore" was used by Greeks in other settings as well. One application was for *mending* a fishing net. Such delicate work requires care to avoid ruining the net. Another use of the word was a medical term as in restoring a broken bone. Note that gentleness is required for restoration in each meaning.

11. What kind of restoration is most needed by the one who is ensnared in sin?
   - Psalm 32:1-5
   - 2 Peter 1:9
   - 1 John 1:8-9

What does it mean to restore with gentleness?

12. Paul warns the Christian who is restoring another, "Keep watch on yourself, lest you too be tempted." How might we be tempted when addressing another person's sins? Consider the

following passages in your answers:
- Ephesians 4:26-27
- Romans 2:1
- Ephesians 6:4

As God's chosen people, He expects us to deal with one another in very specific ways, including when we are in conflict. Reflect on Colossians 3:12-17 as you answer these questions:

13. Why does Paul call us holy and beloved?

14. What should we put on?

15. If we have a complaint against another, what are we called to do?

16. What is to be above all in our overall attitude and action toward one another?

17. What should rule our hearts? In contrast, what else might rule our hearts at times?

18. On what basis ought we teach and admonish one another?

What is the Christian's responsibilities in bringing correction?

It can be frustrating to deal with those who need correction. We may be tempted to argue or even bully the other person into our way of thinking. Or, we may want to avoid any kind of confrontation, denying any responsibility for helping another.

In 2 Timothy 2:24-26, responsibilities are defined for two different roles when correcting others.

19. What are the responsibilities of the Lord's servant?

20. What is God's responsibility and therefore not the responsibility of the Lord's servant?

21. What role should retaliation play in restoration?
    • Romans 12:19

22. In Lesson 5 (question 14), we discussed that forgiveness does not necessarily remove earthly consequences, which may include forms of discipline or making restitution. What is the difference between discipline and retaliation?
    • Hebrews 12:5-6

23. Discuss when you are most tempted to force someone else to repent. What kinds of things do you do? What can you do to help control your passions and avoid taking on God's responsibilities?

24. What is the ultimate purpose of showing someone her sin?
    • James 5:19-20
    • Acts 2:37-39
    • 1 John 1:8-9
    • 2 Corinthians 2:5-8

What if the other person refuses to repent?

Great question! Our Lord anticipated this and gives specific instructions for just such a case.

First, we need to remember what is needed for the person caught in sin. As discussed previously in Question 11, that person needs forgiveness for healing. Thus, the ultimate goal for confronting another about his sin is to restore that person with Christ's forgiveness.

25. What are the dangers for one who is stubbornly unrepentant?
    • Jeremiah 2:35
    • Matthew 11:20
    • Luke 13:1-5
      (For more information, review questions 10 through 14 of Lesson 3.)

In his commentary on Matthew 18, Jeffrey Gibbs notes, "Jesus is teaching about an extreme form of caring, of compassion, of concern for a fellow disciple in a situation of terrible need."[7] Looking at the entire chapter of Matthew 18, Christ stresses the importance of restoring those whose sins are causing them to wander away from God.

26. In Matthew 18:
    - Verses 1-6, whom does Jesus identify as the greatest in the kingdom of heaven?
    - Verses 10-14, whom does Jesus identify as the one in need of care?
    - Verses 15-17, whom does Jesus identify as one in need of special concern?
    - Verses 21-22, how much compassion and forgiveness is required for one who sins again and again?
    - Verse 35, what is the warning for those who refuse to forgive?

27. What does Jesus teach for addressing stubborn unrepentance? Reviewing Matthew 18:

    - Verse 15: Go in _____.

    - Verse 16: Take _____ or _____ others along with you.

    - Verse 17: Tell it to the _____.

    - Verse 18: Treat him as a _____ and a

      _____ _____.

28. Matthew 18:15-20 is sometimes misapplied. What is false about the following assertions?
    - This is a quick three-step process, after which the person should be kicked out of the church.
    - Going one-on-one means a single attempt to let the other person know what he has done wrong (such as sending an email or letter, making a phone call, or even an in-your-face confrontation).

---

7   Gibbs, Jeffrey A. Concordia Commentary: Matthew 11:2-20:34. St. Louis: Concordia Publishing House, 2010. 916.

- Others to bring along as witnesses mean those who agree with you and/or who have authority over the other person and can pressure him to do what you want.
- "Tell it to the church" means broadcasting your accusations, including utilizing verbal gossip and social media.
- Those who are treated as unbelievers should be shunned.

29. Whatever happens, we are called to be faithful to God and His Word. Read Romans 12:18 to answer these next questions.
   - What is our ultimate responsibility?
   - What is NOT our responsibility?

What if the other person is not a Christian?

The Bible's instruction for dealing with someone in conflict applies to both Christians and non-believers. You first go in private to confess your sins, forgive as you have been forgiven, and restore with gentleness. If necessary, you then bring one or two others along, all with the idea of restoring gently. However, the direction to "tell it to the church" does not apply since a non-believer is not accountable to the church.

30. Consider how the following passages apply when relating with non-Christians:
   - 1 Peter 2:12
   - Galatians 6:10
   - Romans 12:14-21

31. Will people take advantage of a Christian who approaches conflict this way?
   - John 15:20
   - Romans 12:14
   - Proverbs 3:5-8

How does restoring others relate to reconciliation?

As noted in Lessons 1 and 5, reconciliation requires confession and forgiveness. Between two people, that usually means mutual confession and forgiveness.

32. We can begin the process of reconciliation by

_____ our own sins, seeking forgiveness.

33. The other person may _____ us as God has forgiven him.

34. We seek to restore with gentleness by helping another see how he has sinned. When the other person repents, we can

proclaim _____ _____, assuring him of his reconciliation to God.

35. We can also _____ the other person as God has forgiven us.

Reconciliation occurs when confession and forgiveness are shared and the relationship is healed.

How is reconciliation related to the Lord's Supper?[8]

The early Christian Church recognized the importance of seeking reconciliation before worship. They took seriously Jesus' admonition in Matthew 5:23-24: "Therefore, if you are offering your gift at the altar and there remember that your brother has something against you, leave your gift there in front of the altar. First, go and be reconciled to your brother; then come and offer your gift."

Addressing their numerous divisions, St. Paul admonished the Corinthians to reconcile. He noted that their disunity was especially offensive as they celebrated the Lord's Supper together (1 Corinthians 10:14-22; 11:17-34). To celebrate the unity we have together in Christ while divisions and factions remain among us is a contradiction of our faith.

---

8   The following section is excerpted from an article by Ted Kober and Eric Sahlberg. See the entire article at www.hisaor.org. Click on "Articles" and select, "Moving from the 'Holy Howdy' to the 'Kiss of Peace.'"

Thus, the believers practiced the "kiss of peace" during their worship. Greeting each other with a holy kiss (see 1 Corinthians 16:20), they shared, "The peace of the Lord be with you." If anyone had difficulty sharing the peace due to unresolved issues, they were urged to reconcile before taking communion.

In earliest Christian liturgies, this practice occurred at the end of the Service of the Word or at the beginning of the Eucharistic section. The purpose: To encourage any who had unresolved conflict to be reconciled prior to celebrating the Lord's Supper at the same table. A form of the "passing of the peace" exists in some of our Lutheran worship services today. In *Lutheran Service Book*, this direction is indicated in Divine Service, Setting 1, after the Prayer of the Church and before the offering:

> Following the prayers, the people may greet one another in the name of the Lord, saying, "Peace be with you," as a sign of reconciliation and of the unity of the Spirit in the bond of peace (Matthew. 5:22-24; Ephesians 4:1-3).[9]

Encouraging worshipers to casually greet one another and meet visitors can be a useful practice, especially in a society where we tend to self-isolate or only talk to those we know. But common niceties cannot replace the necessity to "make every effort to maintain the bond of peace" (Ephesians 4:3) among God's children.

 ## Case Study

As an alternative to reading the following Case Study, utilize Scene 2 from the skit "You Wrecked My Car!" Or, watch the video "Father& Son 2" from the DVD Responding to Sexual Temptation in a High Tech Society. *You can order both the skit and DVD from www.hisaor.org in the bookstore. Note that this is a continuation of the case from Lesson 4.*

17-year-old Matt and his dad just finished fighting about Matt's use of his dad's car without permission. Matt walked out on his father at the end of the argument and went to his room to sulk.

---

9   "Divine Service, Setting One," *Lutheran Service Book*, St. Louis: Concordia Publishing House, 2006. 159.

Matt's father felt guilty about the fight. While he knew he needed to address his son's sins (taking the car without permission; lying about it; treating his father with disrespect), he realized that the manner in which he confronted his son was ungodly. He let his anger get out of control (Ephesians 4:26-27), he called his son various names (Ephesians 4:29), and he provoked his son to anger and failed to discipline him in a loving way (Ephesians 6:4). He failed to show him the love and forgiveness of Christ, even while disciplining him (see Hebrews 12:7-11; 1 Peter 4:8; Ephesians 4:32).

Matt's father took the form *Proclaiming God's Grace* (included with this Bible study) and approached his son's bedroom. Knocking quietly on the door, he asked to come in. Matt responded, "Whatever."

The father began by expressing sorrow over losing his temper and attacking his son. He asked for Matt's forgiveness. Matt quickly responded with "Sure, Dad." This led Matt to admit taking the car, saying that he didn't realize he had damaged it. Matt explained that his friend called, depressed over a breakup with his girlfriend. Matt dropped everything and immediately drove over to pick up his friend and drive around so that they could talk in private.

Matt's dad then introduced him to the form and asked if they could try to confess their sins to God and one another using the pamphlet. Matt agreed. Matt's father confessed first, specifically naming his own sins, asking God and Matt for forgiveness. Using the words of the form, Matt proclaimed God's forgiveness to his father and then offered his personal forgiveness. Matt then confessed his sin to God and his father, identifying some of his particular sins. Matt's father proclaimed God's forgiveness to him and offered personal forgiveness.

Matt ended up paying for the damage to the car. Most importantly, father and son reconciled through mutual confession and forgiveness.

Application Questions

These questions can apply to the above case study or to a current conflict from your personal life. For the case study, assume the father's role. For a conflict from your life, apply these questions to yourself, writing out your answers.

1. How have you prepared to restore the other person with forgiveness? (If you need help with this, review the application questions from Lesson 5.)

2. Before seeking to restore the other person, what kinds of logs do you need to get out of your own eye first (Matthew 7:1-5)? (If you need help with this, see the application questions at the end of Lesson 4.)

3. Review 2 Timothy 2:24-26. What are your responsibilities in helping the person with whom you are in conflict? What are God's responsibilities and not yours?

4. How have you failed to restore the other person in gentleness?

5. Review Galatians 6:1. Identify the sins that you believe have ensnared the other person.

6. If these were your sins, describe what another person could do that would help free you from your entanglement.

7. Identify a time and place that will provide safety for both you and the other person to meet together.

8. Prepare your words by writing out your opening comments.
    * Begin by assuring the other person of your care and Christian love.
    * Acknowledge behaviors and motives of the other person that are godly.
    * Confess your own sins that you have not yet addressed.
    * Next, if you were personally affected, refer to the behavior that caused you personal hurt or harm. Using an "I statement", indicate how you were personally hurt or affected:
        ○ "I feel _____ when you _____ because _____. As a result, I _____."

9. Prepare yourself to listen. The other person will not likely hear anything you have to say until he or she feels that you have listened to him or her. Remember basic skills in active listening:
   - Waiting – Be patient. Wait until the other person finishes speaking before responding. Don't plan your response until the other person is finished speaking.
   - Attending – Maintain eye contact and other body language that communicates your genuine interest. Nod occasionally or respond with short phrases that indicate you are paying attention (e.g., *I see, uh-huh, I understand*, etc.).
   - Clarifying – Ask questions to test your understanding (e.g., *When you said _____, did you mean _____?*).
   - Reflecting – Repeat short portions back to the person. This communicates that you are listening closely and allows for the other person to restate things if needed. It also helps the other person hear back what she has said, which may help her rethink her responses to the situation.
   - Agreeing – Look for opportunities to agree. When you agree with some portions, the other person believes that you are open-minded and really listening. He will much more likely hear what you have to say if he believes you are balanced in your assessment.

10. Prepare open-ended questions to help the other person discover for himself the offensive behaviors and own them. For example:
   - "When you [describe the behavior], what were you hoping would be the result?"
   - "If you had the opportunity, what would you have done differently?"
   - "If someone else had done the same thing to you, how would you have felt?"
   - "Now that you have had time to reflect, what words or actions do you regret?"
   - "What could you have done that would be more reflective of your faith in Christ?"

11. Anticipate the person's reaction to your questions and plan your response.
    - How will you respond if she immediately repents?
    - How will you respond if he becomes angry?
    - How will you respond if she tries to justify what she did?
    - How will you respond if he tries to explain things away?

12. What will be your next steps if he is not yet repentant?

13. How will you proclaim God's forgiveness and then your own?
    - Consider using the form *Proclaiming God's Forgiveness* in which you can both confess and receive forgiveness.

14. Write a prayer seeking God's guidance for both of you.

**Be
Reconciled
to God**

Remember
Whose
You Are

**Be
Reconciled
to Others**

Confess
to the Other
Person

Forgive as
God Forgave
You

Restore
with
Gentleness

Repent
Before
God

Receive
God's
Forgiveness

Leader's Notes

General Instructions

1. Each lesson begins with a review from one of the six chief parts of Christian doctrine as taught in *Luther's Small Catechism*. It is best that the leader not read this entire section for the group, but rather invite one or more participants to read. Participants engage more fully when they are active participants rather than passive recipients. A couple of ways to engage people:
   a. Assign participants to read that section in advance of class.
   b. Ask one or more participants to read that section during class.
   c. If a large group, have people read these sections in small groups.
   d. Use this as part of the opening devotion for each lesson.
   e. The leader could read the questions and the class read the answers.

2. At the end of each lesson is an optional case study with application questions. The case study and application questions may be used in different ways:
   a. For small groups, work through the questions for the case study together.
   b. Divide larger groups into small discussion groups to work through the questions for a case study. Then debrief each group's outcomes for the plenary group.
   c. Assign the case study and application questions as homework. Encourage participants to write out their answers. Then begin your next lesson by discussing some of the answers. Or, a more concise method for reviewing the homework would be to ask, "What did you learn from working through the case study and application questions?"
   d. Rather than the case study, ask participants to consider a specific conflict from their own lives. Ask them to write out their answers to the application questions. If you want to review the homework at the beginning of the next lesson, ask: "As you thought about a conflict in your own life

and reflected on the application questions, what did you learn? I encourage you to use care so that you do not reveal confidences such as identifying others involved in your conflict or sharing information that may be too personal to share. Focus your comments on what you learned that might be helpful for the rest of our class to hear."

e. Use the application questions when coaching someone who is struggling with a specific conflict. You might work through them while together or assign as homework between coaching sessions.

Case Study and Application Questions

For the case study, answers will vary. Direct people back to the Bible verses or catechism reading as needed during discussion.

For true life situations, if someone has difficulty answering application questions (such as question 1 in Lesson 1), he or she should ask for help from a pastor or other spiritually mature person who can guide him or her.

Bible Study Leader's Pack

Ambassadors of Reconciliation offers everything you need to lead a great Bible study including video clips and skits that may be utilized while teaching various sections of the lessons.

Go to www.HisAoR.org, select Bookstore, and search *Go and Be Reconciled Leader's Pack*.

Lesson 1

1. Descriptions and consequences of our sinful nature:
   - A sinful creature.
     - Psalm 51:5. We are sinful from conception, all of us.
     - Romans 3:10-12, 23. None can please God on our own. We all fall short of the glory of God.
     - James 2:10. According to the Bible, even if we fail in one part of the Law, we fail in all of it.
   - An enemy of God.
     - Isaiah 59:2. Our iniquity has separated us from God so that He will not hear us.
     - Romans 5:10. Our sinful nature makes us enemies of God.
   - One who daily struggles with my sinful nature.
     - Job 14:4, 15:14. As humans we are incapable of doing what is right in God's eyes.
     - Romans 7:14-25. We struggle to do that which God has commanded.
     - Galatians 5:17. The desires of our flesh are against the desires of the Spirit.
   - Unclean and worthless, a beggar who has nothing to offer God.
     - Isaiah 64:6. Our righteous deeds are like filthy rags.
     - Romans 3:12. No one does good, not one.
     - 1 Timothy 6:7. We brought nothing into the world and can take nothing out of the world. We are beggars who have nothing good to offer God. We can only beg for mercy and wait on Him.
   - Condemned to be separated from God eternally.
     - Romans 6:23a. The wages of sin is death (eternal separation from God).
2. *Benefits* of our new nature:
   - A new creature through Him.
     - Isaiah 53:5-6. The LORD laid our sin upon His Son so that we can be at peace with God.
     - John 3:16. Those who believe in this gift of God will not perish but will have eternal life.
     - 2 Corinthians 5:16-21. Those who are in Christ are called

new creations. We have been reconciled to God because God put our sin on Christ and Christ's righteousness on us.

- In Baptism changed from an enemy to an heir.
  - ○ Romans 6:2-5. We have newness of life. We have been united with Christ in His death, and we will be united with Him in His resurrection.
  - ○ Galatians 3:26-4:7. We have been adopted as children of God and made heirs of His heavenly promises.
  - ○ Titus 3:5-7. We have hope of eternal life, not because of our works, but because of His great mercy. Now we are heirs according to the hope of eternal life.
- A beloved child of God, precious in God's eyes.
  - ○ Isaiah 43:4. We are precious in God's eyes.
  - ○ John 1:12-13. Through the will of God, we were made to be His children.
  - ○ 1 John 3:1. He lavished His love upon us, calling us to be His children.
- Cleansed and ransomed by the precious blood of Christ.
  - ○ 1 John 1:7. The very blood of Jesus has cleansed us from all sin.
  - ○ 1 Peter 1:18-19. We were ransomed from the slavery of sin, not with gold or silver, but with the precious blood of Christ.
- No longer separated from God. I have been brought near by His blood.
  - ○ Ephesians 2:12-13. Although once separated from Him, those who were once far off have been brought near to God through the blood of Christ.
  - ○ Romans 8:35-39. Nothing shall separate us from the love of God in Christ Jesus our LORD.

3. On my own, I am sinful and unclean, separated from God. But in Christ, I have been made a new creature, an heir of God's heavenly promises, a child of God, cleansed and purchased by Christ's blood. My worth is not measured by my own being or works. Neither is my value defined by what others think. My worth is found in the precious blood of Christ. I am a redeemed child of God!

4. When we suffer from the effects of a serious conflict:
   - Joshua 1:5. God promises to be with us, and He will not leave us or forsake us. We know that God loves us. His promises are sure.
   - Colossians 3:12-17. Thus, we can be compassionate, kind, patient, forgiving – all as God has done for us. As God's chosen ones, we have the peace of Christ in our hearts, and we can put on love. As we let God's Word dwell in us, we can teach and admonish one another with God's wisdom. We can do everything, including how we respond to conflict, in the name of Jesus, giving thanks to God.

5. My Baptism comforts me through the <u>forgiveness</u> of <u>sins</u> and the gift of the Holy Spirit. My <u>sins</u> have been washed away.

6. Baptism gives me my identity as a new <u>creation</u> and a <u>child</u> of <u>God</u>.

7. Baptism reminds me that I am called to live not for <u>myself</u> but rather for <u>Christ</u>.

8. Having been baptized into Christ, I can walk in the <u>newness</u> of life.

9. Baptism teaches me to put off the <u>old</u> <u>self</u> and put on a <u>new</u> <u>self</u>.

10. Making the sign of the cross reminds me that I have been baptized into God's Triune name and given a new name – Child of God.

11. Making the sign of the cross adjusts my attitude to remember whose I am: Christ's. I have been purchased and won through His blood. I am a forgiven child of God, called by Him to live a new life.

12. First, I need to be reconciled to <u>God</u>.
    - Psalm 51:3-5. My sins are against God, and I have sinned against Him.
    - 1 John 1:8-9. I need to confess my sins to God, who forgives me and cleanses me from all unrighteousness.

13. Next, I need to be reconciled with others:
    - Matthew 5:23-24. Someone who has something against <u>me</u>.
    - Matthew 18:15. Someone who has sinned against <u>me</u>.

14. I may need to help a brother or sister who is <u>caught</u> in sin. (Note: The original Greek word for "caught" is meant as a fish

caught in a net or an animal ensnared in a trap. Such a fish or animal cannot free itself – it needs help.) However, I must use care to restore in a spirit of gentleness so that I also may not be <u>tempted</u> to sin.

15. We should view others in conflict as people for whom <u>Christ has died</u>.

16. My most serious conflict in all of life is with <u>God</u>.

17. The consequence of being in conflict with God is <u>death</u> (i.e., eternal separation from God).

18. In addressing my conflict with Him, God chose <u>reconciliation</u>.

19. *Reconciliation* is usually considered more difficult because it requires confession and forgiveness. People would rather deal with the material issues than have to face the humility of confession or to forgive someone who has sinned against them.

Lesson 2

1. Desires (or passions) that wage war in our hearts describe the internal battle between doing what is godly and doing what is sinful. Our selfish desires conflict with God's desires for us. They are designed to serve ourselves before God or others. Ultimately, these represent our desire to be god or like God, which was the temptation the devil used in Genesis 3:5.

2. Our fights and quarrels begin with our desires to serve ourselves rather than God or others. Ultimately, we want to be the god of our own lives. Such selfish desires lead us to sin against God as well as others.

3. Each sinned against the 1st Commandment by making demands upon others as if he or she was "god." They each sinned against other commandments as follows:
    *   Teenager: 4th, 5th (notice the definition of murder in Matthew 5:21-22 and 1 John 3:15), 8th, and 10th (coveting) Commandments.
    *   Worker: 4th (honoring authority), 5th, 7th (she was stealing by taking work time away from employer), 8th, and 10th Commandments.
    *   Husband: 2nd, 5th, 6th (not loving and honoring his wife), 8th, and 10th Commandments.
    Note that each of the three could have expressed disagreement in a godly way but instead chose sinful methods to express their disapproval when they did not get what they wanted.

4. Sin originates in the heart.

5. Three ways we sin against the First Commandment:
    *   Fearing someone or something more than God.
    *   Loving someone or something more than God, which in the Bible is called a craving or lust.
    *   Trusting someone or something more than God, which could be called misplaced trust.
    It is not necessarily sinful to fear, love, or trust someone or something other than God. We sin when our fears, love, or trust for created things is greater than our fear, love, or trust in God.

6. These three things become idols because we fear, love, or trust in them more than God. In our hearts, they replace God, and thus we make them false gods.

7. Cravings
   - 1 John 2:15-17. Loving the world more than God. Desires of the flesh, desires of the eyes, and pride of life.
   - Galatians 5:16-21. Gratifying the desires of the flesh, which are against the desires of the Spirit. Works of the flesh: sexuality, immorality, impurity, sensuality, idolatry, etc. Note especially descriptions of what we do in conflict: enmity, strife, jealousy, fits of anger, dissensions, divisions, and envy.
   - Ephesians 4:17-20. Futility of the mind, darkened in understanding, alienated from the life of God. Callous, sensuality, greedy to practice impurity.

8. Answers will vary. Improper desires for physical pleasure might include sexual desires (that we attempt to fulfill in ways other than God instructs), eating to an excess, sleeping or resting more than is healthy, drinking too much, and taking drugs illegally.

9. Note that the 9th and 10th Commandments are often broken in desires that become idolatrous. We often fail to honor authorities when we demand our way, which is sin against the 4th Commandment.

10. Consequences:
    - Proverbs 8:13. Pride and arrogance are ways of evil; God hates perverted speech.
    - Proverbs 16:18. Pride leads to destruction and a fall.
    - Matthew 23:12. Those who exalt themselves will be humbled.

11. James calls them a judge. In his question, "Who are you to judge your neighbor?" the inferred answer is a self-proclaimed "god."

12. In gossip, we puff ourselves up by tearing down someone else and harming their reputation. This is a sin against the 8th Commandment.

13. Gossip is a sin against the First Commandment because we set ourselves up as judges with the right and position to

judge and condemn others. Instead of trusting God most of all, we trust our own judgments and punishments (hurting others' reputations) rather than God. In other words, we make ourselves god.

14. Dangers
- 1 Timothy 6:10. Dangers include all kinds of evils, including wandering away from the faith and piercing themselves with many pangs.
- Hebrews 13:5. Dangers include being discontented with what you have, which could lead one away from being content with God and what He promises.

15. Answers will vary.

16. *Fear of man* vs. *Fear of God*
- Proverbs 29:25. Fear of man is a snare, but He who fears (trusts) the LORD will be safe.
- Luke 12:4-7. Man may be able to kill the body, but the Lord can destroy both the body and the soul. We need not fear man more than God because we are valuable to our Lord. Note Psalm 130:4.

17. Answers will vary. If people need help, give the example of a 17-year-old Christian boy who is invited to a party where no adults are around and drugs and alcohol are offered. He is tempted to take the drugs and alcohol so that he will be liked by the people at the party and invited again, even though he knows it's wrong. Peer pressure is an example of fear of man.

18. Ways to recognize when good desires turn into idols:
- Luke 12:22-31. A good desire includes being concerned about the necessities of life (e.g., food, clothing, shelter) so that we plan and work to provide for ourselves and our families. However, worry or anxiety reveals our lack of trust in God to provide what we need. Our lack of trust in God, that is, our idolatry, is revealed when we get angry, say hurtful words, or find other ways to punish those who don't give us what we want.
- James 4:1-3. Desires in and of themselves are not idolatrous. In fact, many desires are godly. However, when we fight and quarrel to get what we want, our good desires have turned into demands, and we are guilty of idolatry. Instead of

trusting that God will provide everything we need, we take it upon ourselves to get what we want, when we want it, and how we want it.

19. Answers will vary. Note that good desires can become idolatrous when we demand that we have them our way. This may include such things as wanting successful children, a well-paying job, leisure time, a loving spouse, etc. If people need additional examples, review the previous examples with the teenager, worker, and husband.

20. Answers will vary.

21. Jonah 2:8. Those who hold on to their idols eventually forfeit hope in God's love.

22. 1 John 5:21. Avoid idolatry.

23. She sacrificed her integrity, her witness to Christ, and her reputation. The allure of idolatry is that by sacrificing to it you will gain something desirable. The deception is that you lose something valuable and gain nothing good.

24. Answers will vary.

25. Psalm 51:17. God requires a broken spirit and a contrite heart.

26. Comfort for our sins and hope for overcoming temptation:
   • Psalm 51:1-12. In this prayer of repentance, we pray in faith knowing that God answers us for His Son's sake. God cleanses us through forgiveness. He creates in me a clean heart, renews a right spirit within me. He does not cast me away from Him or take His Holy Spirit from me. He restores to me the joy of His salvation and upholds me with a willing spirit.
   • 1 John 1:9. God forgives us and cleanses us from all unrighteousness, which includes the idols of our hearts.
   • 2 Corinthians 5:14-15. Christ died for us so that His love controls us. He gives us power to live for Him and not just for ourselves.
   • 1 Peter 2:24. Because Christ bore our sins on the cross, we can die to sin and live for righteousness. His wounds bring healing to us.

Lesson 3

1. Covering up one's sins:
   - David summoned Uriah for giving a report of the battle, then sent him home to spend time with his wife before returning to battle. When David learned that Uriah refused to go home, he delayed Uriah so that he could have him attend a banquet. The king caused Uriah to get drunk and sent him home a second time. Once again, Uriah did not go home. So David gave Uriah a message for Joab, ordering that Joab place Uriah in a position where he would be killed in battle. David believed that people would assume that Bathsheba's pregnancy was the result of her husband being home from battle, and thus the secret of his affair would be protected.
   - Proverbs 28:13 teaches that those who conceal their sins will not prosper.
2. David's sins were numerous:
   - He was guilty of pornography (continuing to watch Bathsheba bathe rather than turning away, feeding his sexual lust), which is a form of adultery (see Matthew 5:27-28).
   - Misusing his authority as king by summoning Bathsheba to him.
   - Adultery – Having relations with another man's wife.
   - Misuse of authority and betrayal – Knowing her husband was Uriah and that Uriah was serving the king in battle; he betrayed the trust of a faithful soldier and of an entire nation. This was a misuse of his authority as king.
   - When he learned Bathsheba was pregnant, he made several attempts to cover up his sin rather than confess.
   - Murder – Arranging for Uriah's death in battle.
   - Arrogance and pride – In spite of all that he had done, he married Bathsheba. He assumed that his own way of covering up his sin had taken care of things.
3. Although we don't know David's heart, his actions suggest he may have been guilty of worshipping a number of idols:
   - Improper desire for sexual pleasure – He watched Bathsheba

    bathe, increasing his lust for her. He then had sexual relations with her, knowing that she was married to Uriah.

- Pride and arrogance – He misused his authority to satisfy his own sexual lusts. He attempted to self-justify by covering up his own sin. He acted like God by having Uriah killed in battle. He married Bathsheba as if he had done nothing wrong.
- Love of money and material possessions – If he was honest with God and his people, he would have confessed his sin and may have lost these things. Instead, he attempted to cover up his sin in order to protect his wealth.
- Fear of man – Fearing loss of reputation and respect of people rather than fearing God most of all.
- Good things he wanted too much – This included desiring his own good reputation, power, control, position as king, self-justification, pride, satisfying sexual desire, etc.

4. David sacrificed his relationship with God, the respect of Bathsheba and Uriah as individuals, the respect of Uriah for his service to the king, and his own reputation as a godly leader. He potentially risked his entire kingship. As consequences, he lost the son born to Bathsheba, and the sword never departed from his house.

5. Just as David denied his sin, we at times deny our sin. As David tried to cover up his sin, we sometimes do the same. One lie must be followed with others. We trust our own sinful ways to deal with our sin, instead of trusting God and His ways. Before we realize it, our sinful reactions are spiraling. We sacrifice to our idols. Others are hurt because of our sin.

6. 2 Samuel 11:27. The LORD was displeased.
2 Samuel 12:13. Yet God still loved David, showing him great mercy, sparing his life, not taking away his kingship, and forgiving him.

7. We often suffer consequences of denying our sin, much as David did. The longer we deny our sin, the worse the consequences become, including hurting others.

8. Nathan engaged David through a story that he knew would touch the king's heart. David had been a lowly shepherd boy and would recognize the injustice of Nathan's story.

9. Through David's confession and God's forgiveness

(absolution) announced by Nathan. This is an example of private confession and absolution.

10. "The Truth" is defined as <u>Jesus</u>.

11. "The Word" is defined as <u>Jesus</u>.

12. When we deny our sin, we deny our need for Jesus. We justify ourselves. Those who justify themselves deny their need for the Savior. Denial of sin is a denial of faith in Christ. This is dangerous! Note that those who remain in manifest unrepentance are to be treated as unbelievers.

13. Jesus warns about those who self-justify:
    * Matthew 9:10-13. The Pharisees in their judgments acted as if they were righteous on their own deeds (self-righteous). The self-righteous do not need a Savior. In response, Jesus declares that He came to call sinners, not the "righteous" (or, the self-proclaimed "righteous").
    * Matthew 23:27-28. Although they may appear righteous to others, they are full of hypocrisy and lawlessness.

14. Depending on our own good deeds for righteousness:
    * Isaiah 64:6-7. We become like one who is unclean. *All* our righteous deeds are like a polluted garment (refers to a cloth used for a woman's menstrual period, which was a time of uncleanness).
    * Luke 18:9-14. When we trust in ourselves that we are righteous, we become like the Pharisees who exalted themselves and put others down. Jesus concludes, "Everyone who exalts himself will be humbled, but the one who humbles himself will be exalted."

15. What led to his righteousness was his humility and confession, begging for God's mercy.

16. Good News:
    * Proverbs 28:13. He who confesses obtains mercy.
    * 1 John 1:9. God is faithful and just to forgive us our sins and to cleanse us from all unrighteousness.

17. Stand before God and not be condemned:
    * 2 Corinthians 5:21. God put all our sin on Jesus and Jesus' righteousness on us. Because we are covered in the righteousness of Christ, we can stand before God and not be condemned.
    * Romans 1:16-17. We are righteous by faith in Christ Jesus.

- Romans 8:1. Therefore, because we are in Christ Jesus, we are not condemned.

18. All who believe in God's only Son Jesus will be saved from eternal damnation and have eternal life.

19. Those who do not believe in Jesus are condemned already, because they do not believe in the name of the only Son of God.

20. Contrition is "terror smiting the conscience with a knowledge of sin." Before giving the answer to how contrition is minimized, allow participants time to think and respond. In our culture, we minimize sin by avoiding calling sin what it is, by dismissing it (*It's not that bad!* or *Don't worry about it!* or *No problem!*), or by calling it a mistake (or a miscalculation or an error in judgment). We have focused on Jesus as our friend and brother at the expense of the holiness and almightiness of God. Many believers today have forgotten the true fear of the Lord (see Proverbs 1:7 and Matthew 10:28).

21. The second part is faith in the Gospel of Christ and the forgiveness of sins (absolution). This faith in our forgiveness delivers us from the terror of sin and its consequences.

22. Answers will vary. Allow time for participants to respond.

23. Good works are the fruit of repentance.

24. Because we sin daily, daily contrition is necessary.

25. As we confess our sin, believing in the forgiveness we have in Christ, we confess our faith in our Lord and Savior.

26. Christ's forgiveness empowers us to die to sin and live for righteousness.

27. People do not bear good fruit when they become nearsighted and blind, forgetting that they have been cleansed from their former sins.

28. Means God has given us:
    - Corporate <u>confession and forgiveness (or absolution)</u>
    - Private <u>confession and forgiveness (or absolution)</u>
    - Confession and forgiveness with a <u>brother</u> or <u>sister</u> in Christ
    - The <u>Word</u> of God
    - The <u>Lord's Supper</u>
    - Remembering my <u>Baptism</u>

    Note: The written and spoken Word of the Gospel and the sacraments are the means of grace. Absolution (proclaiming God's forgiveness) is the spoken Word of the Gospel.

Lesson 4

1. She may not trust him with the car or trust his promises. She may resent him for his disrespect. Her reputation has been harmed with the dentist, and her pride may be hurt.

2. His sister Amy has been affected. Her dentist has also been inconvenienced by James' irresponsibility. Whomever the dentist needed to meet has been affected. And, anyone who learns about James' lateness (or his mother's) or their fighting with one another (probably through slandering comments).

3. James' mother sinned in response to her son's sins:
   - Galatians 6:1-2. She failed to restore her son with gentleness, and thus, she was also tempted to sin in her response.
   - Ephesians 6:4. Through her angry response, she provoked her son to anger. She failed to exemplify firm yet loving discipline and instruction in the Lord.
   - James 3:1. As his mother and an authority figure, she is responsible as a teacher to be a good example. Instead, she lowered her standards and imitated her son's immature and sinful behavior.

4. He justified himself by blaming his mother for her failures. Her sins against him do not justify his sins against her and others. Only Christ can justify James (1 John 1:9).

5. While James denies his sins, he denies his need for a Savior. He is guilty of sinful pride and a self-righteous attitude. For more information on this answer, review questions 10-12 from Lesson 3 and the corresponding answers in the Leader's Notes.

6. Once he realized how late he was, he should have immediately confessed his sin, asking for forgiveness and accepting full responsibility for the consequences of his actions and inactions. Regardless of what his mother does, he is responsible for initiating reconciliation by confessing his sins (see Romans 12:18; Matthew 5:23-24; James 5:16). He should have not responded disrespectfully to his mother, especially since he sinned against her and others by being late.

7. James can be comforted:
   - Proverbs 28:13. In confession, he will find mercy – whether

or not from his mother, certainly from his God.

- 1 John 1:9. God forgives and purifies us from all unrighteousness.
- 1 Peter 2:24. Jesus bore James' sins on the cross that James might die to sins and live for righteousness. By Christ's wounds, James has been healed.

8. James should confess his sin to God, his mother, his sister, the dentist, and any others he learns have been harmed by his sins.

9. The mother should confess her sins, trusting in God's forgiveness for her:

- James 5:16. She should confess her unloving confrontation to her son. She can do so without taking away the need to restore her son for his sins.
- Matthew 5:23-24. God calls her to initiate reconciliation. She is especially responsible as a teacher to model reconciliation (James 3:1).
- 1 Peter 2:24. Christ bore her sins on the cross for the forgiveness of her sins.

10. Answers will vary. Some verses include:

- Psalm 32:1-5; 103:1-5, 8-13; Psalm 133
- Matthew 5:9; 6:12, 14-15; 11:28
- Colossians 3:12-15
- Ephesians 1:7-8
- 1 John 1:7; 3:1
- See also the list of verses in the answer to question 17 of this lesson.

11. Hurtful words naturally come out of our mouths, rather than words that are helpful for building up and giving grace to those who hear them.

12. Our sinful words grieve the Holy Spirit of God.

13. Our Lord calls us to put away all bitterness, wrath, anger, clamor, etc.

14. God loves us, forgiving us in Christ, showing us undeserved kindness and compassion. He calls us to do the same for one another.

15. Use of anger:

- Psalm 30:4-5. God's anger is short-lived, but His joy and forgiveness are forever.

- Psalm 103:8-13. The LORD is slow to anger, abounding in steadfast love and mercy for His children. He does not keep His anger against us forever, but instead lavishes His love on us through the forgiveness of our sins. He demonstrates His compassion for us.

16. Our anger should not last longer than sunset (less than a day!). Otherwise, we are likely to give the devil an opportunity to tempt us to sin.

17. Other dangers:
    - Proverbs 14:29. One with a hasty temper exalts folly.
    - Proverbs 15:1. A harsh word will stir up anger.
    - Proverbs 22:24-25. Scriptures warn against being friends with a man who gives in to anger; we may lose friends or respect of others because of our uncontrolled anger. People in leadership may lose their position or influence.
    - James 1:20. The anger of man does not produce the righteousness of God.

18. We demonstrate faith in ourselves for righteousness. In other words, we are guilty of self-righteousness and self-justification. This is a sin against the 1st Commandment, since we essentially place ourselves above God. Our actions indicate that we believe more in ourselves than in Christ and His forgiveness.

19. Who is responsible for initiating reconciliation?
    - Matthew 5:23-24. Each Christian who knows someone has something against him or her. This may mean approaching someone to ask what one has done to cause offense and, if convicted, to begin by confessing.
    - Matthew 18:15. Anyone who has been sinned against.
    - Romans 12:18. All Christians are called to live at peace with everyone. Thus, every Christian is called to initiate reconciliation, no matter who may have caused offense. According to the Bible, two Christians who are in conflict should approach each other for peacemaking. God's plan is that both will come to seek one another. However, in our sinful world, neither may be willing to initiate the process. Nonetheless, both are individually responsible to "go and be reconciled."

20. Mutual confession and prayer leads to healing. Remember that confession includes both acknowledging one's sins and receiving the forgiveness of sins.
21. The words "I'm sorry" may mean:
    - The person is expressing godly sorrow for his/her sin.
    - The first person is sorry that the other person is hurt, but not necessarily acknowledging that the first person is responsible in any way.
    - The person is sorry that he/she will suffer consequences as a result of what has happened (worldly sorrow).
    - The person is sorry that this is such a big deal.
    - The words "I'm sorry" may precede justification or blame shifting (*I'm sorry, but…* or *I'm sorry if…*).
22. Two kinds of sorrow or grief:
    - Worldly sorrow or grief
    - Godly sorrow or grief
23. Worldly sorrow may be an expression of being unhappy about the consequences that may be suffered (e.g., "I'm sorry I got caught" or "I'm sorry that I have to make restitution"). Godly sorrow is expressed when one acknowledges how he has sinned against God and others and has harmed others. Godly sorrow is also expressed when one is willing take responsibility for the consequences (e.g., the prodigal son in Luke 15:18-19 or Zacchaeus in 19:8). Two of Jesus' disciples illustrate the two kinds of sorrow or grief. Both grieved their betrayal of Jesus:
    - Judas, who took his own life demonstrated worldly sorrow (Matthew 27:3-5)
    - Peter, who repented and was forgiven by Christ demonstrated godly sorrow (Matthew 26:75 and John 21:15-19)
24. An apology can be an excuse (e.g., "I apologize – please excuse me") or a defense (e.g., *The Apology to the Augsburg Confession*). Also see the answers to question 21 for using the words "I'm sorry." Most of these fail to express that the one apologizing is wrong. "Apologize" is not a biblical substitute for confess.

    Nevertheless, saying "I'm sorry" may be appropriate for good manners as a way of saying, "Please excuse me." For example, we might say "I'm sorry" when we sneeze or need to move past someone. In our society, we are conditioned to make no distinction between confessing sin or using polite manners.

25. Guidelines for Confession:
    - Go as a <u>beggar</u>.
    - <u>Own</u> your sin. ("Confess" is appropriate here, but "own" has the sense of assuming full responsibility.)
    - Identify your sins according to <u>God's</u> <u>Word</u>.
    - Express <u>sorrow</u> <u>for</u> <u>hurt</u> your sin has caused.
    - Commit to <u>changing</u> <u>your</u> <u>behavior</u> with God's help.
    - Be willing to <u>bear</u> <u>the</u> <u>consequences</u>.
    - Ask for <u>forgiveness</u>.
    - Trust in <u>Christ's</u> <u>forgiveness</u>.

26. Guidelines included in the confession to God:
    - Go as a beggar (calling on "most merciful God" and confessing we are by nature sinful and unclean. We justly deserve God's present and eternal punishment. We have nothing to bring but can only beg for mercy).
    - Own your sin ("We have sinned against You in thought, word, and deed, by what we have done and by what we have left undone. We have not loved You with our whole heart; we have not loved our neighbors as ourselves").
    - Identify your sins according to God's Word (not loving God with our whole heart and not loving our neighbors as ourselves is a reference to Commandments listed in several places, such as is summarized in Mark 12:30-31).
    - Commit to changing your behavior with God's help ("renew us, and lead us, so that we may delight in Your will and walk in Your ways to the glory of Your holy name").
    - Ask for forgiveness ("For the sake of Your Son, Jesus Christ, have mercy on us. Forgive us...").
    - Trust in Christ's forgiveness (our confession to God indicates our trust in His forgiveness, which we then receive in the Absolution, the proclamation that our sins are forgiven because of Jesus' death on the cross).

27. Whether or not the other person is a Christian, the believer is called to the same responsibilities in confession. The "Guidelines for Confession" still apply, although one might be careful how he identifies sins according to the Bible,

using more general references rather than specific Bible verses. However, the one confessing should not expect an unbelieving person to respond with forgiveness. How can an unbeliever forgive as God has forgiven him? Confessing sin to an unbeliever in this way may be so different from what the unbeliever has experienced that he may ask the one confessing about that kind of response. This gives the believer an opportunity to give reason for the hope he has in Christ (see 1 Peter 2:12).

Lesson 5

1. Biblically false or weak:
- Excusing: Sin is never "okay." Sin is never "no problem." Saying "don't worry about it" ignores the seriousness of sinning against God and others.
  - Isaiah 59:2. Our sin separates us from God – that's not okay!
  - Romans 6:23a. The wages of sin is eternal death – it's a serious problem!
  - James 2:10. Even if we think we have only sinned in one small way, God says we will be held accountable for the whole law – we need to be concerned about all sin!

  Note: Excusing sin is sin.
- Punishing:
  - Luke 6:36-37. We are called to be merciful. We are warned against judging and condemning others or we will be judged and condemned. Instead, we are called to forgive and we will be forgiven.
  - Romans 2:1. When we judge others, we condemn ourselves because we are guilty of the same things. Although we often don't think of it that way, God does.
  - James 4:11-12. When we judge and condemn our neighbor, we are playing God. Only God has the right to judge and condemn.
- Earning:
  - Romans 6:23b. The free gift of God is eternal life in Christ Jesus, through whom we are forgiven.
  - Romans 5:15. Because Christ died for us, we have the grace of God and the free gift of grace that *Christ earned* for many.
  - Ephesians 2:8-9. We have been saved by grace through faith. This is not a result of our own good works. None of us can boast that we have earned our forgiveness and salvation.

  We do not deserve God's forgiveness. We can do nothing to earn it – forgiveness is a free gift. If we are to forgive as God forgives, then we cannot expect others to deserve or earn our gift.

- Recalling:
  - Jeremiah 31:34. God promises not to remember our sins.
  - Psalm 103:8-10. In God's abounding mercy, He does not keep His anger against us forever. He does not treat us as our sins deserve or repay us according to our iniquities.
  - 2 Corinthians 5:17, 21. God sees us as a new creation. We have the righteousness of Jesus and are no longer judged by our sin.

2. Note how God forgives me:
   - God's justice required <u>blood</u>.
     - Hebrews 9:22. Without the shedding of blood there is no forgiveness of sins.
     - 1 John 1:7. Jesus' blood purifies me from all sin.
   - Christ <u>paid</u> the full price for my sins.
     - Isaiah 53:5-6. Christ was pierced for our transgressions, crushed for our iniquities. The chastisement that He suffered brought us peace and healing. All we have been like sheep who have gone astray, but God put the sins of the whole world upon His Son.
     - John 19:30. When Christ said, "It is finished," He meant that our entire debt had been paid in full.
   - My forgiveness is <u>not conditional</u> upon my works.
     - Romans 6:23b. God's gift of eternal life in Christ Jesus is free.
     - Ephesians 2:8-10. We are saved by grace through faith. None of this grace is based on our own works. None of us can boast that our works save us. But our redemption makes us His workmanship, created in Christ Jesus, so that we can do the good works that God planned for us to do.
   - My past sins will not be <u>brought up</u> and used against me.
     - Jeremiah 31:34. God does not "forget" my sins, but He chooses not to remember them. Thus, He promises not to bring them up again.
     - 1 Corinthians 6:11. Although we were once considered sinful and unworthy of God's grace, we are now viewed by God as washed, sanctified, and justified in the name of Jesus and by the Spirit of our God. This washing reflects our Baptism.

- My sins do not <u>condemn</u> me.
  - John 3:17. Jesus did not come to condemn sinners including me, but to save them including me.
  - Romans 8:1. Those in Christ Jesus are not condemned.
- I am covered by Christ's <u>righteousness</u>.
  - Romans 3:21-22. We who believe have the righteousness of God through faith in Jesus Christ.
  - 2 Corinthians 5:21. God made Jesus, who had no sin, to be sin for us, so that we would become the righteousness of God. Christ exchanged our sin for His righteousness.

3. Christ warned that if we do not forgive others their sins, our Father in heaven will not forgive our sins.

4. Jesus did not mean that our forgiveness is dependent upon our good works, including forgiving others. God's forgiveness is a free gift, as we saw in the earlier passages. However, if we refuse to forgive others as God has forgiven us, we self-righteously act as though we do not need God's forgiveness. This is an act of unbelief. Those who remain in a state of unbelief reject the free gift of God. Thus, those who refuse to forgive demonstrate their faith in self-justification and deny their need for Christ. Those who do not believe that they need Christ and His forgiveness are condemned (John 3:18). They retain their own sins and are not forgiven. (Note questions 10-14 in Lesson 3. Those who deny their own sin justify themselves and deny Christ and His forgiveness.)

5. Answers will vary. By nature, we are not loving and forgiving as our heavenly Father is. As sinners, we struggle to forgive on our own strength. To forgive is divine. It requires divine power, which God promises His people (see 2 Peter 1:3-4). But what is impossible for man is possible with God (note Mark 10:27 and Philippians 4:13).

6. What do I demonstrate in forgiving others?
- That I believe in my own <u>forgiveness</u> of <u>sins</u>.
  - Acts 10:43. I am forgiven because I believe in Jesus.
  - Ephesians 1:7-12. I am redeemed through Jesus' blood, forgiven because of the riches of His grace.
  - Colossians 3:12-13. I am chosen by God, holy and beloved. As one who is forgiven, I can thus be compassionate, kind,

humble, meek, patient, bearing with others and forgiving others.

- That I believe that Jesus died for the sins of <u>all</u> <u>people</u>.
  - ○ Luke 23:34, 42-43. Jesus prayed for the forgiveness of those who crucified Him. My sins, and the sins of all other people, are responsible for Jesus' crucifixion. In verses 42-43, Jesus promised the believing criminal next to Him that he would be with Christ in Paradise. This in spite of the fact that the man was a criminal who was sentenced to death on a cross and had no opportunity to amend his sinful life and perform various good works.
  - ○ John 3:16. God loved the whole world and gave His Son for all. Those who believe this good news are saved from condemnation.
  - ○ Romans 3:23-26. Just as all have sinned, all are justified by the redemption in Jesus Christ.
- That I remember that I am a forgiven <u>child</u> <u>of</u> <u>God</u>, saved by His grace.
  - ○ John 1:12-13. God gave believers in Christ the right to be called His children. They are born of the will of God.
  - ○ 1 John 3:1. God lavished His love upon us and called us to be His children.
  - ○ Ephesians 1:7. We have the forgiveness of our sins, by grace, which God lavished upon us. Through Christ, we have obtained an inheritance as His children.
- That I am a <u>disciple</u> <u>of</u> <u>Jesus</u> who loves others as God <u>loves</u> <u>me</u>.
  - ○ John 13:34-35. All people will know that I am a disciple of Jesus by how I love others, just as Christ has loved me.
  - ○ 1 John 4:10-12. We are called to love one another because God loved us. As we love one another, we demonstrate that God abides in us and His love is perfected in us.
  - ○ 1 Peter 4:8. We are admonished to love one another because love covers a multitude of sins (forgiveness is a form of love).

7. What we demonstrate when we fail to forgive others as God has forgiven us:
   - Matthew 18:21-35. God will treat us as we treated others. In

the parable of the unmerciful servant, we are exhorted to forgive as God has forgiven us.

- 2 Peter 1:9. We are nearsighted and blind because we have forgotten that we were cleansed from our past sins.
- Colossians 3:12-13. We have failed to clothe ourselves with the qualities God calls us to, including bearing with one another and forgiving as God has forgiven us.

In summary, we demonstrate weak faith in the forgiveness of our sins. Unforgiveness can separate us from God.

8. What power or abilities does God promise to give His children?
- Ephesians 3:14-21. God grants us strength through His Holy Spirit so that we may live our lives in faith and so that we may have strength to comprehend the immensity of God's love. Thus, we will know the love of Christ and be filled with all the fullness of God. The Holy Spirit works through the means of grace (His Word and Sacraments).
- 1 Peter 2:24. Because Christ died for us on the cross, we can die to sin and live to righteousness. Through Christ's wounds, we are healed.
- Philippians 4:13. With the Apostle Paul we can confess, "I can do all things through Christ who strengthens me."

We cannot on our own strength forgive as God does, but God promises to empower us to do what He commands. When we struggle to forgive, we should confess our weak faith and ask God to enable us to forgive as He has forgiven us.

9. Why does neither of these viewpoints present a biblical perspective?
- "No mercy" – God himself is merciful and gracious, slow to anger and abounding in steadfast love (see Psalm 103:8). He requires us to do justice, to love kindness (mercy), and to walk humbly with God (see Micah 6:8). So consequences may be appropriate, but that does not remove our responsibility to forgive as the Lord has forgiven us (see Colossians 3:13; Ephesians 4:32).
- "Forgive and forget" – Forgiving does not mean forgetting. Neither does it mean that there will be no earthly consequences. Consequences may be required by justice,

especially to make restitution. See question 14 for the godly purposes of consequences.

10. Forgiveness always relieves the consequence of eternal separation from God.
    - Romans 6:23. Forgiveness relieves us from eternal death.
    - Romans 8:1. Those who are in Christ Jesus are not condemned.

11. After leading the Israelites for 40 years, Moses could see the earthly Promised Land but was not allowed to cross over into it with his people.

12. Moses appeared on the Mount of Transfiguration. Note that while he could not enter the earthly Promised Land, he did enter the eternal Promised Land. (He was forgiven, although there were earthly consequences.)

13. Regarding King David:
    - 2 Samuel 12:13. David was forgiven by God as proclaimed by the prophet Nathan.
    - 2 Samuel 12:10-12, 14. David's consequences included the sword never departed from his house, one who was close to him (his son) openly had relations with his wives, and the son born to Bathsheba and David died.

14. Purposes of consequences:
    - May be necessary to provide restitution.
        ○ Numbers 5:5-7. God commanded that when someone committed a sin, he should confess and make full restitution plus a penalty for his wrong.
        ○ Luke 19:8. The fruit of Zacchaeus' repentance was to pay back "fourfold" to anyone he defrauded.
    - May be a form of discipline for teaching the sinner.
        ○ Proverbs 3:11-12. The LORD disciplines those He loves, just as a father reproves a son he loves.
        ○ Hebrews 12:11. Discipline, which may be unpleasant, is a form of teaching which yields the peaceful fruit of righteousness.
        Note: The root word for "discipline" (and for "disciple") is derived from the Latin *disciplina* meaning instruction given, teaching, or learning.
    - Provide others an example or warning.

- ◦ 1 Corinthians 5:-6-7. If there are no consequences for a publicly known sin, it may give the impression that the sin is not that bad. Others may be encouraged to sin in similar ways. On the other hand, consequences for publicly known sins serve to discourage others from sinning.
  - ◦ Acts 5:5. When Ananias was punished for his sins, "great fear came upon all who heard it." People properly learned to fear God more than trusting in their own idols.
- May protect a sinner from further <u>temptation</u>.
  - ◦ Matthew 6:13. In the Lord's Prayer, we pray "that God would guard and keep us so that the devil, the world, and our sinful nature may not deceive us or mislead us into false belief, despair, and other great shame and vice" (from explanation to the Sixth Petition of the Lord's Prayer, *Luther's Small Catechism*, quoted at the beginning of Lesson 5). God sometimes uses consequences to help protect us from future temptation. For example, when a teenager wrecks the family car because he was careless, his driving privileges may be revoked until he can prove his trustworthiness. (He may also need to pay for damages, a form of restitution.)
  - ◦ 1 Thessalonians 4:3-8; 5:22. God calls us in sanctification to abstain from sexual immorality, to avoid those things that tempt us. Consequences that remove such temptations from us protect us. In 5:22, Paul calls us to avoid every form of evil. A consequence may help us in this endeavor.

15. The disciples asked, "How many times must I forgive?" Jesus answered seventy-seven times (varies by translation).
16. The number is not limited to 77 or 490 – seventy times seven (varies by translation). He meant that the number is unlimited.
17. When did or does God forgive me?
    - Romans 5:8. While I was still a sinner.
    - 1 John 1:9. When I confess my sin.
    - Matthew 26:26-28. In the Lord's Supper.
    - Acts 22:16. When I was baptized.
    - 1 Peter 2:24. On the cross.
    - Genesis 3:15. In the garden, when the promise was made to Adam and Eve.

- Ephesians 1:4. Before the foundation of the world.

18. Why is not everyone going to heaven?
    - Because those who do not believe reject His gift of forgiveness and are condemned.

19. Why do we confront another about his sin?
    - Mark 1:15. So that the person may repent and believe in the gospel, the good news that for Christ's sake his sin is forgiven.
    - James 5:19-20. If a sinner does not repent, he is in danger of wandering away from the truth and losing his soul. The brother who confronts his sin will save him from eternal death, covering a multitude of sins.

    We confront another about his sin so that God might bring him to repentance and he may believe that he is forgiven. We prepare him to receive the gift that is already his in Christ Jesus! (See 2 Timothy 2:24-26; John 3:16-18; Romans 5:6-11)

20. The disciples asked Jesus to increase their faith, recognizing that it takes faith in Christ to forgive as God has forgiven us.

21. Instruction from Scripture when resolving material issues:
    - Proverbs 16:1-3. It is important to plan but necessary to commit those plans to the Lord.
    - Philippians 4:5-6. Be reasonable, knowing that the Lord is near. Don't be anxious, but pray.
    - Matthew 22:39. Love your neighbor as yourself.
    - Philippians 2:3-5. Look not only to your own interests but also to the interests of others. Have the mind of Christ as you negotiate.
    - Philippians 2:14. Do everything without grumbling or disputing.
    - Proverbs 12:15. A wise person listens to sound advice. Seek godly counsel to assist you.

22. Final instruction:
    - Philippians 4:8-9. Focus on those things that are honorable, just, pure, lovely, commendable, and excellent. Practice what God teaches in His Word, and the God of peace will be with you. Remember that the context for Philippians 4:2-9 is a significant disagreement between two women in the church (v 2).

Lesson 6

1. A person's sin harms his relationship with God:
   - Isaiah 59:2. Sin separates one from God so that He will not hear him.
   - Romans 8:7-8. Sin indicates that one is hostile to God. The person who lives in the flesh cannot please God.
   - James 1:14-15. Sinful desires lead to spiritual death, that is, eternal separation from God.
2. Unresolved conflict harms the church in which the parties belong:
   - 1 Corinthians 1:10-11 – It creates division within the church. 1 Corinthians 3:1-4 – It gives evidence of spiritual immaturity. Jealousy and strife are from the flesh and demonstrate human behavior, not maturity in Christ. 1 Corinthians 10:16-17 – Because we all participate (share, fellowship) in Christ's body and blood, we are one with Christ and one together in Christ. Unresolved conflict makes a mockery of the unity we have in Christ.
   - Galatians 5:13-15. Failure to love one another and biting and devouring one another lead to destruction. Unresolved conflict will eventually destroy the church.
   - Philippians 4:2-3. Paul wrote about the conflict between two women to the entire church because their division affected the entire body. The familiar verses that follow (Philippians 4:4-9) instruct the church in how to address this conflict.
3. Unreconciled relationships affect our witness:
   - John 13:34-35. People will know we belong to Christ if we love one another. If we fail to love one another, as demonstrated in unreconciled relationships, others will not know that we truly belong to Christ.
   - 1 Corinthians 6:4-8. When Christians take other Christians to court, they fail to give witness to Christ and His forgiveness. Paul says such Christians are defeated already because they wrong and defraud one another.
   - 1 Peter 2:12. We are to keep our conduct among unbelievers honorable so that they will learn about Christ and eventually believe in Him. If we fail to reconcile with

fellow Christians, we fail in our witness to Christ and His atoning work in us, that is, the ministry of reconciliation (2 Corinthians 5:16-21).

4. Those who remain unreconciled yet commune at the same altar discredit the unity Christians have together in Christ. Such actions serve to undermine their personal confession of faith in Christ, and they diminish the witness of the church.

5. How does the Lord's Supper strengthen us?
   - Matthew 26:26-28. The Lord's Supper strengthens us through the forgiveness of our sins, including the sins of failing to love others and forgive as we have been forgiven.
   - 1 Corinthians 11:26. In the Lord's Supper, we proclaim His death until He returns. 1 Peter 2:24. Through Christ's death on the cross, we are empowered to die to sin and live for righteousness.
   - Philippians 4:13. In faith, we receive Christ's body and blood in communion. What we cannot do on our own strength, we can do through Christ in us.
   - 2 Corinthians 5:14-15. Christ's love controls us. He died for us, that we might no longer live only for ourselves but also for Christ. Receiving Christ's body and blood in faith fills us with His love, moving us in fervent love toward one another.

6. The one who is "caught" in a transgression needs to be restored.

7. Those who are spiritual are called to restore with gentleness the one "caught" in sin.

8. Others who need to be restored and by whom:
   - Matthew 18:15. The one who sins against you needs to be restored. (Note: Some scholars question whether the words "against you" should be included based on certain manuscripts.) You (addressed to Christians) need to go and restore him.
   - Philippians 4:2-3. Euodia and Syntyche were two women who needed restoring because they were in a significant disagreement. Paul called upon a fellow believer in the church to help the women "agree in the Lord." This applies to us today when two people in the same church are in conflict. They first are to be encouraged to reconcile on their

own; if they are unable, another from the church is called to assist them.

- James 5:19-20. Anyone who wanders from the truth needs restoring. The one who restores is "whoever" from among the believers. That includes you and me.

9. An ensnared animal may be hurting and will be fearful and defensive. It may try to defensively attack anyone helping it.

10. Those who help a brother ensnared in sin must intentionally use care. The one ensnared may be hurting or angry, and he may act out of fear or defensiveness. He may lash out at anyone helping him, especially if he feels attacked. He will respond best to someone who is able to demonstrate a genuine desire to help with understanding, love, and care.

11. What is needed most by one who is ensnared in sin is forgiveness from God, which cleanses us from our unrighteousness. This healing restores our relationship with God and opens the door for restoring our relationship with others:

- Psalm 32:1-5. The sinner needs relief from the oppression of guilt. Blessed healing (restoration) comes when he confesses his sin to God and receives His forgiveness.
- 2 Peter 1:9. He needs to remember that Christ's forgiveness cleanses him from all sin, thereby providing comfort and curing his spiritual blindness (restoring his spiritual sight).
- 1 John 1:8-9. He needs to confess his sin, thereby confessing his need for Christ, and receive the forgiveness that has been won for him on the cross. Through confession and forgiveness, the sinner is cleansed from all unrighteousness (restoring his relationship with God).

12. When restoring another, we might be tempted:

- Ephesians 4:26-27. To let our anger get out of control, thus giving the devil a foothold in our lives.
- Romans 2:1. To sinfully judge the other person in a condemning way when we ourselves are guilty of the same thing. In so doing, we condemn ourselves.
- Ephesians 6:4. To provoke our children to anger rather than bring them up in the discipline and instruction of the Lord.

13. We are holy and beloved because we have been reconciled in Christ's body by His death as we continue steadfastly in the faith (Colossians 1:22-23).

14. We are to be clothed with compassionate hearts, kindness, humility, meekness, and patience (see also Galatians 5:22-23 for fruit of the Spirit).

15. We are called to forgive others as we have been forgiven.

16. Our overall attitude and action should be to put on love, which binds everything together in perfect unity.

17. The peace of Christ should rule our hearts. This peace results from our reconciliation to God through the blood of Christ's cross (Colossians 1:20). This contrasts with our Old Adam nature to serve our own desires above others (see James 4:1-3; Philippians 2:3-4).

18. We should teach and admonish one another with all wisdom based on the word of Christ, which should dwell in us richly. If we are not regularly in God's Word, we will fail in this responsibility.

19. The responsibilities of the Lord's servant include:
    - Not be quarrelsome,
    - Be kind to everyone,
    - Able to teach,
    - Patiently endure evil (challenging to do when working with difficult people),
    - Correct opponents with gentleness.

20. God's responsibility is to grant repentance leading to a knowledge of the truth. It is not the responsibility of the Lord's servant to make another person repent.

21. Retaliation is not part of restoration. Note, however, that discipline or earthly consequences may be necessary (see next question).
    - Romans 12:19. We are not called to avenge ourselves but rather trust in God's judgment.

22. The root word for "discipline" means learning (see Lesson 5, Leader's Notes for question 14, for more extensive discussion of discipline including restitution).
    - Hebrews 12:5-6. One way our heavenly Father exhibits His care for us as His children is through loving discipline.

Discipline is done for a person's welfare, not harm.
Retaliation is done to bring harm to another person, not for
their welfare.

23. Answers will vary. Things that people do to force repentance
may include exercising uncontrolled anger, making threats,
becoming vengeful, developing hatred, punishing the person
with one's own sinful behavior, etc. To help control these
passions, I should look to Jesus (Hebrews 12:1-3), reflecting
the mind of Christ who humbled himself for my sake
(Philippians 2:1-8), seeking His help (Philippians 4:13), and
remembering my own forgiveness in Christ (2 Peter 1:9).

24. The ultimate purpose of showing someone her sin is to
proclaim God's forgiveness to her, leading to healing, comfort,
and restoration. Showing one her sin prepares her for receiving
the Gospel. This is reflected through the following:

- James 5:19-20. Saving a wandering soul from death and
covering a multitude of sins (forgiveness).
- Acts 2:37-39. Leading her to repent and be baptized, for the
forgiveness of sins.
- 1 John 1:8-9. Leading her to set aside denial, to confess, and
to be forgiven in Christ.
- 2 Corinthians 2:5-8. Forgiving her, comforting her, avoid her
being overcome by excessive sorrow, and for affirming love
for her (God's and yours).

25. Dangers for the stubbornly unrepentant include:

- Jeremiah 2:35. God will bring to judgment those who deny
their sin.
- Matthew 11:20. Jesus denounced cities where the people did
not repent.
- Luke 13:1-5. Jesus warns that if we do not repent, we will
perish.

Note that in Lesson 3, questions 10-14, we reviewed how
denying one's sin is to deny one's need for Christ. Those
who justify themselves profess to have no need for a Savior,
which is an act of unbelief, leading to spiritual death.

26. In Matthew 18:

- Verses 1-6. Jesus identifies those who humble themselves
like children as the greatest in the kingdom of heaven.

Children are dependent on and trust in some authority figure who cares for them. Child-like faith is evidenced in humble dependence upon Christ.

- Verses 10-14. Jesus directs us to seek after and care for the one who wanders astray, much like a single sheep that leaves a flock of one hundred. The ninety-nine are left in order to focus on providing care to the one who is wandering.
- Verses 15-17. Jesus instructs us to provide special concern for one who sins, intensifying efforts for one who refuses to listen to loving correction. The instruction begins privately. If there is no repentance, the special concern increasingly involves others over time.
- Verses 21-22. We are to forgive without limitation the one who repeatedly sins.
- Verse 35. Unforgiveness of others is a demonstration of lack of faith in one's own forgiveness from Christ. Thus, by their actions, those who refuse to forgive reject their own forgiveness from God.

27. Addressing unrepentance in Matthew 18:
    - Verse 15. Go in <u>private</u> ("between you and him alone").
    - Verse 16. Take <u>one</u> or <u>two</u> others along with you.
    - Verse 17. Tell it to the <u>church</u>.
    - Verse 18. Treat him as a <u>Gentile</u> and a <u>tax collector</u> (in other words, treat him as one who does not trust in Christ nor believe his own need for the forgiveness of sins).

28. Matthew 28:15-20 is sometimes misapplied. What is false about the assertions?
    - This is NOT a quick three-step process for getting rid of a problem person, but it is rather for restoring him as a believer in Jesus. This requires a great deal of time, love, forbearance, and patience. The unrepentant person's eternal welfare is at risk.
    - Going one-on-one does NOT mean a single attempt to confront someone, regardless of the media utilized. Furthermore, Jesus instructs us to "go" to the other person – in other words, face-to-face. (Consider how you want others to approach you when you are the one needing restoration.) The Greek verb tense translated "go" means to keep on

going. The private attempt to restore should be exhaustive. Only when the person refuses to listen should one begin to involve others.

- Others to bring along as witnesses does NOT mean those who agree with you or have authority over the other person. The others you bring should be people that you both respect and trust. You need to be open to their counsel as well. After all, you might be wrong in your assessment! (Remember the warning in Galatians 6:1.)

- "Tell it to the church" does NOT mean broadcasting your accusations, and it certainly does NOT mean gossiping through verbal communication or social media. "The church" refers to the local congregation which has responsibility for its members' spiritual health. It does not mean to tell the whole church on earth! (Note that posting accusations on websites or social media is also broadcasting to non-believers.) Since the purpose is to restore a wandering soul, "tell it to the church" is to remain as private as possible as long as possible. It begins with involving the congregation's spiritual leadership. If the person continually demonstrates unrepentance, then that person's congregation treats him as an unbeliever. This is done so that he might comprehend the seriousness of his lack of repentance, hopefully leading him to repent and be restored as a fellow believer. The purpose for such a process continues to be restoration.

- Treating someone as an unbeliever does NOT mean to shun the individual. Remember how Jesus treated unbelievers. He didn't avoid them – He loved them, socializing with them. He called them to repent and believe in the Gospel. Nevertheless, those who demonstrate manifest unrepentance are to be excluded from participating in the Lord's Supper because they justify themselves, demonstrating lack of faith in their need for Jesus' forgiveness. Those who do not believe in Christ's forgiveness for them must not be allowed to participate in communion because such participation brings judgment on them (1 Corinthians 11:27-29). However, they are to be the object of our evangelism. They are people who are in desperate need of the Gospel.

Note: When a sin against someone reflects a significant abuse of authority, or when someone would be in physical danger by confronting another, safety for those in harm's way must be considered. For example, if a child is sexually molested by an adult, you do not send that child alone to confront the abuser. Another person needs to be involved to provide protection (including from authorities), not only for that child, but possibly for others who may be vulnerable. We need to keep in mind God's commands to protect those who cannot protect themselves, such as orphans and widows (see Exodus 22:22-23; Psalm 82:3; James 1:27). At the same time, the one who is accused must be given just opportunities to defend himself against false allegations.

29. In Romans 12:18:

  - "...so far as it depends on you, live peaceably with all." Our ultimate responsibility is to do everything possible to live at peace with everyone. We are responsible for our own attitudes and actions. This includes going directly to the other person, confessing our own faults, forgiving others as God in Christ has forgiven us, restoring with gentleness, and involving others as Scripture teaches.

  - "If possible, so far as it depends on you...." We are NOT responsible for what others think or do. Thus, we are not responsible for making someone repent, confess, forgive, or love.

30. The following passages apply when dealing with a non-believer:

  - 1 Peter 2:12. Act with godly integrity, no matter how unbelievers respond, so that in the end they may see what you have done and be moved by your witness to believe in Christ. When a Christian approaches conflict with humility, patience, personal confession, forgiveness, and the like, such behaviors make a powerful witness to the difference Christ makes in one's life. Because these actions are so different than what people expect, unbelievers may ask why a person would do such things. This provides the Christian with the opportunity to share the difference Jesus makes in his life.

- Galatians 6:10. Do good to everyone. In spite of what may happen, the child of God is called to keep His commandments and follow Jesus' teaching, whether with believers or unbelievers.
- Romans 12:14-21. Our thoughts, proactive actions, and responses to others are not dependent upon their thoughts, actions, or responses to us. Rather, we are called to respond to conflict in ways that reflect our faith in Jesus Christ. The last verse of this section summarizes: "Do not be overcome by evil, but overcome evil with good."

31. Yes, it can happen, just as it can with other Christians. But we do not respond to conflict biblically just for the purpose of getting the result we want. We remain faithful to Christ and His teachings because of what He has done for us and promises us. We then entrust the results to God, who is the ultimate judge and Savior.
    - John 15:20. Jesus tells us we will be persecuted just as He was.
    - Romans 12:14. When we are persecuted, we are to bless and not curse.
    - Proverbs 3:5-8. We are exhorted to trust in our God and not in our own ways.
32. We can begin the process of reconciliation by <u>confessing</u> our own sins, seeking forgiveness.
33. The other person may <u>forgive</u> us as God has forgiven him.
34. When the other person repents, we can proclaim <u>God's forgiveness</u>, assuring him of his reconciliation to God.
35. We can also <u>forgive</u> the other person as God has forgiven us.

Notes

CPSIA information can be obtained
at www.ICGtesting.com
Printed in the USA
FSOW04n0053190416
19285FS